# KEEP ON ROLLIN

### From Owning One of the Largest Bus Lines to Damn Near Sleeping In One

*Sammie R. Armstrong*

## Sam Armstrong

### With Trish Geran

Keep On Rollin: From Owning One of the Largest Bus Lines to Damn Near Sleeping in One.
Copyright © 2022 by Sammie Armstrong

ISBN: 9798836267353

Narrated: Sam Armstrong
Written: Trish Geran
Edited: Susan Pence
Cover Design: Trish Geran & Sam Armstrong

Armstrong, Sammie "Sam": 1942-

Biography
1. Armstrong, Sammie "Sam" from Lisbon, Louisiana
2. Life and times in Lisbon, Louisiana during 1940s
3. First Black owned bus line in Las Vegas 1980s-1990s
4. Owning property on Las Vegas Boulevard in 1980s
5. History of the crossing guards in Las Vegas in 1970s
6. Blacks in all-White community in 1965
7. The effects of the Watts Riot in Las Vegas
8. Transportation to the Nevada Test Site in 80s-'99
9. Employee at Pepsi Cola in Las Vegas during 1960s
10. Greater Las Vegas Buffalo Soldiers 9th & 10th Cavalry

# KEEP
# ON
# ROLLIN

**From Owning One of the Largest
Bus Lines to Damn Near
Sleeping In One**

# Dedication
# &
# Acknowledgements

This book is dedicated to my family, friends, kids and grandkids. Thank you for continuing to be a bright spark in my life.

To all of my former employees of Ray & Ross Transport. My intentions were to create a family atmosphere and you helped me to do just that.

To Douglas McCain, Elgin Simpson, Susan Pence, Vickie Monroe, Jackie Brady and Jim Kaufield, who were there at the beginning, thank you for your invaluable support and hard work.

To the Greater Las Vegas Chapter Buffalo Soldiers 9th & 10th Cavalry, thank you for being such an inspiration. It has been a pleasure educating the community about the history of these courageous and fearless soldiers, and I will never forget the hayrides we had with the kids.

To Bishop Clinton House and First Lady Dr. Mary House of Mountain Top Faith Ministry and Minister Aubrey Branch; Deacon Sam Coleman, Deacon Wesley and the entire Deacon Board, thank you all for your invaluable spiritual guidance and friendship.

# Contents

This little light of mine
I'm going to let it shine
Oh, this little light of mine
I'm going to let it shine
Hallelujah
This little light of mine
I'm going to let it shine
Let it shine, let it shine, let it shine

Ev'ry where I go
I'm going to let it shine
Oh, ev'ry where I go
I'm going to let it shine
Hallelujah
Ev'ry where I go
I'm going to let it shine
Let it shine, let it shine, let it shine

—Old Negroe Spiritual

"In his heart a man plans his course,
but the Lord establishes his steps."
—Proverbs 16:9 NIV

# CHAPTER ONE
# A MILLION MILES AWAY

I was born in a small town called Lisbon, Louisiana. Yeah...I hadn't heard of it either until my parents told me about it. All I knew was it's not too far from Monroe, and when I was born, the population was about 200 and it's still about that today.

In 1944, when I was two years old, my mom and dad packed up our belongings and took me and my 10 siblings to Camden, Arkansas for a better life. But then again, that was the same reason they moved from another little town in Arkansas called Wilmot.

Wilmot is about 94 miles from Lisbon. It was where my mom, Annie White, and Dad, George Armstrong, met while picking and chopping cotton on a plantation for a White man. She was 13 and he was a little older, and in between working in the fields and traveling back and forth came us kids.

I was the second youngest of 12, eight boys and four girls. There was Ester Lou (1920-2002); Mattie "Little Mattie" (1924-1988); William "Buck" Henry (1924-1967); Willie "W.C." Cloud (1927-1987); Velma Lee (1930-2017); twins Walter Hugh (1933-1982) and George Jr. (1933-2007); Eva Mae (1937-2015); Bobby "Bill" Eugene (1938-2009); and James Allen (1940-1966). It's hard to believe that Billy Gene (1946-Present) and myself are the only two left today.

We were all born by way of a midwife except for Billy. My mom had complications during the delivery so he was born in the local hospital for Colored patients. There would have been more of us but three were lost during the delivery, which was common in families during that time period.

I never asked my parents why they had so many kids, but if I had to guess, family represented survival and the greater the number, the more hands there were to help out with the chores in the fields and around the house. It was a sure way to keep food on the table and clothes on our backs.

After a few years of working in Lisbon, things were going okay until my dad was told that he would have to start paying the cost to have the cotton seeds removed at the gins. He did it a few times, but when he didn't get reimbursed, he packed up and moved the family to Camden, Arkansas, which was about 69 miles north.

The move to Camden seemed more promising mainly because there were ten times more people who lived there than where we had just relocated from. We moved into a house owned by a White man named Cap Man, and for income, my dad would borrow money to harvest crop and then repay it after he sold all of it. He was what you would call in those days, a sharecropper.

Around a year later, my mom and her sisters, Aunt Lee and Aunt Mattie, who also lived there, decided to pool their monies and purchase 13 acres of land so they could build a home and own a piece of the American dream. Aunt Mattie was in charge of the transaction, and when it came time to divide the properties amongst the sisters, she claimed eight acres and gave Aunt Lee and my mom two and a half. At first, my dad thought Aunt Mattie took so much and gave so little because she was the oldest and she thought she was entitled. But regardless of the rift, we built our house and eventually discovered a well connected to a spring, just down the hill from the house, so our house had running water. By this time, my dad was a farmer and his heart was in the soil.

On Sundays, we would put on our "Sunday Best" and attend the local Baptist church, but as soon as we hit the door we had to take them off and put on our work clothes. My mom would prepare a full course soul food dinner and sometimes the preacher would join us at the table. Some families didn't allow the kids to be present during this time, but my dad insisted we be there.

Shortly after we were all moved in our homes, Aunt Mattie decided to build a church and a house for her son that we would later find out was partially on our property. She had sure enough crossed the line this time and my dad was some kind of mad. She tried to justify her decision but in his eyes it was still called greed and it caused a wedge between our families that was never removed. But even though Dad barred her from coming over, I found no reason why I shouldn't continue to walk down to her house and play with my 13 cousins.

**"One of the tests of leadership is the ability to recognize a problem before it becomes an emergency."**
**— Anonymous**

# TIME FOR SCHOOL

My mom went as far as the eighth grade so she knew how to read and write. On the other hand, my dad's level of education was never discussed. He could not write but he could count; in fact, he was great at it. But regardless of what they lacked, they made sure we at least were given an opportunity.

My first day of school wasn't at all what I expected. Believe it or not, my kindergarten class was the inside of a restaurant. Since their customers came in around five o'clock in the morning to eat and didn't return until later that evening, the owners felt that the space and time could be used as a classroom for teachers.

When I went to "real" school, which was 1st to 6th grade at Northside Elementary, it was located two miles from my house. My parents didn't want me walking that far so they arranged for my brother W.C. to pick up me and my two brothers, James and Bobby after school. W.C.'s job was chopping puff wood and then hauling it to the paper mills. Boy did I love riding in the back of his Puff Wood Truck.

Northside was segregated and the books we were taught from were hand-me-downs from the White schools, which was common, especially in the south. The pages were torn and the main topics were scribbled which made it virtually impossible to fully understand the lesson that was being taught.

When I was 10 years old, I worked in the fields from sun up to sun down for $3.75 a day, chopping cotton in its early stages and pulling the weeds out which was necessary for adequate growth. For as long as I live, I'll never forget

Mom Annie White and Dad George Armstrong
Pictured in background is my brother's
Puff Wood truck

The house where I grew up in Camden, Arkansas

those hot scorching summers when it seemed like the humidity was higher than the temperature outside.

After I finished Northside, I attended Lincoln Junior High School. In addition to taking the basic classes (reading, writing, arithmetic) I enrolled in a woodshop class, and the skills I learned in there became a passion. And I continued to enroll in that class as long as it was offered.

Lincoln High School was where me and my brothers James and Bobby became interested in sports. We all made the football, basketball, and baseball teams and went to practice faithfully after school. But regardless, my dad made arrangements with the district for me, and only me, to pick up garbage after school. It was so embarrassing.

My buddies and football teammates (Lewis McGee, Charles Reed, Lee Lee Green, and George Scott) knew that I dreaded being seen as the garbage man, especially by the girls, so they came to my rescue. They walked along side me picking up the scattered debris, and all of a sudden the job didn't seem so demeaning anymore.

Ninth grade would prove to be a pivotal time in my life. I had an argument with my dad and decided to move out of the house and in with my sister Velma Lee. That was my home until I finished high school.

On Saturday mornings, it was a family ritual to sit on the front lawn and have quality time. The boys would take turns mowing the grass, but my dad asked me to do it for three consecutive Saturdays and I wasn't having it. When I told him it was one of my brother's turn, he looked me in the eye and said, "You do it!" I said that I would not. Then he asked my brothers James and Bobby to go and get a switch. James went in the house and Bobby, the agitator, went to get one. I ran into the woods and hid for two days. My mom got so worried, she sent my sister Velma to look for me.

After getting beat three times with a razor strap and a horse whip, I made a promise to myself that I wasn't going to take it anymore. They started when I was 10 years old, when I was blamed for letting the wagon get in front of the horses, and all I knew was that it was time for a change.

Velma took me in like I was her son. My brother W.C. would come over to check on me and to make sure things at school were going okay. During his visits, I started to realize that he was not just being a big brother, he was becoming my mentor.

Ever since James and Bobby started playing football, I felt that my dad respected me less and favored them more. I played baseball, football, and basketball but I guess that didn't matter. I even ran track and was a high jumper.

After I left home, I would go back on family quality time day to see my mom and the rest of the family and my dad would be there. He wouldn't say a word and neither would I.

One day, while sitting in the cafeteria at school, a friend told me that Grady Wilson was beating up my brother James. I broke the glass of the fire extinguisher box, grabbed the hatchet and rushed over to where the fight was going on. I took one swing at Grady and nicked his ear. When it started to bleed, I came to my senses and realized that I could have cut off his ear or killed him and suffered the consequences for the rest of my life for no legitimate reason. I would find out later that the fight was over a girl named Muerine. She was dating James and Grady at the same time.

In high school, I played whatever position the coach wanted me to play. For football, it was tight end both offensive and defensive; basketball it was forward; and for baseball I played every position except for pitcher. In those days, when a player sustained an injury, which in my case was more than likely from playing football, I was told to place a bag of ice or a hot towel directly on the area or walk it off.

My friend Lewis McGee was the quarterback for Lincoln High School and we were both captains of the team. Coach Little, from Tennessee A&I College, now called Tennessee State University (TSU), had been interested in recruiting us ever since we were in eighth grade. He would call our house and ask how things were going but he never came to see us play.

During our senior year, Coach Little finally made a visit to Lincoln and he brought three scholarships. I was 6'1" and weighed 130 pounds and Lewis was around the same. He looked us up and down and said, "You two are way too small to play for Tennessee. Shoot, we have guys on the sidelines who weigh 225 pounds." Lewis and I looked at each other as if to say, "Well, I guess that's that."

After graduating from Lincoln High School, Lewis went on to play for Auburn State. I placed my dream of becoming a football player on the shelf and decided to leave Arkansas to visit my brother James in Las Vegas, Nevada.

L-R: Lewis McGee, me, and Lee Lee Green

L: James, me, and Bobby

# CHAPTER TWO
## A BUMP IN THE ROAD

James worked at a hand car wash in Las Vegas. And as soon as I stepped off the bus, in 1961, I started to work alongside him. One day, a cute girl in a clean looking Cadillac came in for a wash. She said her name was Marilyn and the car belonged to her momma, but I didn't care because my attention was on her. I knew the moment she drove away, that somehow, some way we would meet again.

At that time, my mind was still on playing football. I wasn't ready to hang up my cleats and I sure wasn't going back to Arkansas. Coach Little might have thought I wasn't big enough but my desire was, and it became even stronger after experiencing that humiliating rejection. My goal was to play on the level of Cleveland Browns legendary running back Jim Brown, so I could see my name in lights.

My Aunt Mattie had relocated to Ontario, California, which was about 39 miles from the University of Southern California (USC), the school I had my eye on. Ever since I read how the school gave Willie Wood an opportunity to become the first Black quarterback to play in the PAC-12 Conference in the late 50s, I thought maybe the doors were open for more Black players. So I bit the bullet and took a hell of a risk to live with Aunt Mattie as a walk-on recruit for the USC football team.

Three of Aunt Mattie's grandkids lived with her; one was a senior at Chaffey College (a two year college) and the other two had graduated from there. Aunt Mattie had a janitorial business and we were all expected to work. My schedule was already tight trying to make the football team, but she didn't care.

I would get up at 6:00 a.m. and hitch-hike a ride to school. After practice, which was around 4:00 p.m., I cleaned houses and businesses. I had no time to study. I concentrated on football and my body felt every bit of my conflicting worlds.

Living with Aunt Mattie came with a price. She only gave me orders on what to do and not once did we hold a decent conversation. She never made a negative or positive comment about my plans to play football, but instead, she would call the folks back home and gossip about how much of a burden I was. It cut like a knife but I chose to lick my wounds and overlook the discomfort of living under her roof and pray that I make the team so I could say *thank you* and *goodbye.*

I will never forget attending the USC Trojan's football orientation. It was the closest to my dream I'd ever been. John McKay was the head coach and he was warm, charming, and had this remarkable way of relating to his players. We felt special just being in the same room with him. Before Coach McKay was named the head coach a few years back, in 1960, he was an assistant. And on the offensive line was a notable assistant named Al Davis, the future NFL owner of the Las Vegas aka Oakland Raiders.

One day, Coach McKay arranged to meet with the Black players, and I will never forget his words of wisdom. He said:

> I never want to see any of you guys walking by yourself. Each time I see you, I want at least two of you together. I never want to see more than five of you at a time together. Because if they catch you by yourself there are no witnesses. If they see five or more of you together they will call you a gang. If you're driving a car, especially at night, and they pull you over, drive slowly into a shopping center where there are a lot of people. Always try to have a witness.

Of course, all of us knew that he was talking about the White racist people who might try to harm us just for the fun of it. Most of us were already told that if the police stopped us while driving, to place our hands on the steering wheel in the eleven and one o'clock positions and to not move when they asked to see our license and registration.

Football practice was so long and exhausting, there were days when I thought about playing dead. After a few weeks of the loss of blood and sweat, I decided to have a talk with Coach John McKay about my chances of making the team. He suggested I play for Chaffey College first, learn the ins and outs and sharpen my skills and then come back and try out. He said that a lot of his players who came from there earned starting positions.

Coach John McKay was the first White man who talked to me with respect and who didn't make me feel like I was lesser than he was.

Chaffey was a junior college located in Rancho Cucamonga and it was only about six miles from Aunt Mattie's house in Ontario. I decided to trust his words and advice and enroll in the "Home of the Panthers".

After school, I would go to practice and then work for Aunt Mattie's janitorial service. When I got home, I was too tired to study and I started to wonder how all of what I was doing was going to work out. I had no end game, only a dark cloud above my head.

Aunt Mattie finally made one call too many, complaining to my mom that I was nothing more than another mouth to feed, that I was wasting my time and she didn't want me there. My mom immediately sent my brother James to get me and told him to take me back to Las Vegas and help get me settled.

In those one and a half years in Southern California, I learned a lot but it was time to let go of my dream and get real about moving on.

L-R: Jimmy Hegler, me, and Bernard Lee Westbrook, my high school math teacher and football and basketball coach

I've always been headstrong. I liked football because the few NFL players we had were making a lot more money than the baseball players in the major league. The lights were brighter for them and people really bragged about them. Jim Brown and Baltimore Colts quarterback, Johnny Unitas were household names. And when Jim quit playing football because he wanted to be treated on the same playing field as the White players, this decision meant the world to me.

"God, grant me the serenity to
accept the things I cannot change,
the courage to change the things
I can, and the wisdom to
know the difference…"
—Reinhold Niebuhr

# CHAPTER THREE
# A TURN IN THE MIDDLE

The year was 1963 when I moved to Las Vegas. Three years before my arrival, segregation in the hotels and casinos and public places was no longer allowed. But the Westside was the area of town where Blacks had been designated to live and continued to do so even after Jim Crow supposedly left town.

James rented a "spot" in a two bedroom apartment at 909 Washington Avenue from our sister Ester's daughter, Juanita Walker, who also lived there. There were eight of us crammed in there like sardines and it became uncomfortable. James moved out, but I decided to stay because there was a girl I had my eye on in the complex.

James was the manager at a full-service (gas) station on H Street and Owens Avenue called Chief Cut-um Price and it was within walking distance from where I was staying. The owner, Jack Casey was a White man from Oklahoma who I think was part Native American. He named the station after a prominent Chief in his hometown who left a mark of excellence on his heart and Cut-um Price was one of them. I later found out that he was personally acquainted with quite a few notable Native Americans back home.

James hired me to be a service station attendant. So when a car pulled up, my duties were to fill the tank, check the tire pressure, fluids and oil, and wash the car's windows. If they needed a road map or anything for their car, they could get them inside our store. James collected the money and if he was pre-occupied, I would do it.

The drive-thru service stations began to disappear in the 1970s because the Arab-Israel War imposed an embargo against the United States which caused an oil crisis. It led to a panic. Consumers looked for the lowest price and the station with the least overheard expense could offer it.

James (above) and me taking inventory at
Chief Cut-um Price Service Station

When I was working at Chief Cut-um Price, gas was $.25 per gallon. During the 1970s, it was $.36.

On the job as a service station attendant at
Chief Cut-um Price

I finally saved enough to move into my own apartment on D Street and Jefferson Avenue, but what I really wanted was to move into a house. I didn't have an interest in working in the casinos because I didn't like punching a clock and someone standing over me, so I started to feel doubtful about my move to Vegas and the possibility of owning my own home. I wanted to get away from that mentality of master vs. slave as soon as possible. How and when-I had not a clue.

Then one day, one of my customers, a White man named Bill came in and said that because of the new integration "law", Pepsi Cola wanted to diversify by hiring Black workers. He worked there and said that it would be worth pursuing a position. And I agreed.

When I interviewed for the job Bill had suggested, there was only one Black in the office. His name was Frank and he was the janitor. When I went back to the station, I got a call and was told I had the job and I could start as soon I wanted. **I became the second Black to work for the PepsiCo, Inc. in Clark County, Nevada.**

At first, the company was privately owned by a Mormon named Leonard Bennett and it was simply called Pepsi Cola Bottling Company Las Vegas. But when the national branch of Pepsi bought the company, Bennett was given a position in management and the corporate office brought in a man named Mr. Dunleavy to run the company.

The first person I thought to tell my good news to was Jack Casey. He wished me lots of success and said the door was open if I decided to come back.

Jack was the second White man who treated me like I was a human being not like a Black man who worked for him at a gas station. Today, the Casey family owns the Phillips 66 stations in Clark County, a chain of general stores, and gas stations all over the country.

# CHAPTER FOUR
## A PLACE TO CALL HOME

At Pepsi, I started working in the warehouse, loading the trucks and taking inventory. Then I was promoted to forklift operator and shortly after became the Water Treatment Specialist. My job was to make sure the water purification equipment and clean water was stored and available where ever it was needed. I continued to work at the gas station because I enjoyed the type of customers we attracted and it was nice to run into familiar faces. Plus Jack and James were a great bunch of guys to work for.

Around this time, my friend Douglas (Doug) McCain, who worked as a stand-by bus driver for the Clark

County School District, told me they were looking for drivers and suggested I add the position to my resume. I placed the idea on the back shelf and told him I would get back with him about it.

Mr. Dunleavy and I were on good terms and every so often he would call me on my days off to do repairs around his house. A few times, he called me in his office and asked if I felt that the Black employees which was still only the janitor and me, were being treated equally. I told him that Mr. Bennett was hard to work for but other than that, I really didn't see a big difference.

Leonard Bennett was a short red-neck looking man, and my height (6'1") didn't intimidate him whatsoever. He reminded me of someone who had no respect for Blacks, and in fact, I would bet he only cleaned up his language in the workplace because he had to.

He wasted no time criticizing me for everything that went wrong during my shift. When the bottles were over filled, it was my fault. If they tipped over, it was because I wasn't paying close attention.

Regardless of the constant harassment on the job, in 1965, I bought a house for $12,000 in an all-White neighborhood on Brady Street, which was near Washington Avenue and Bruce Street. At that time, Las Vegas, like most major cities, was going through social changes; some were for the best and some were not. I felt proud, like a pioneer when I signed on the bottom line. I always believed that owning property allows you long lasting wealth and plays an uplifting role in the community. I felt self-sufficient and at the same time a little skeptical about making those $99 a month payments.

I had planned to move in the following weekend but then the Watts Riot broke out. My real estate agent, William "Bob" Bailey suggested I wait until the racial tensions, which were happening all over the country and in Vegas, calm down.

The people in Watts, a neighborhood in southern Los Angeles, were tired of the constant mistreatment by police officers, and housing discrimination. Black people rebelled by looting and burning buildings in their communities. In Vegas, on the Westside, most of the stores in the Golden

West Shopping Center were sacrificed and cars were turned over on residential streets.

After four days of rioting, Bob called and said to come by his office to pick up my keys and that it was time for me to move into my new and first house.

A few days after I moved in, I went to work and Mr. Bennett wanted to know why in the hell would I want to buy a house in a White neighborhood and where did I get the money. He knew about my plans because he had to verify my work status for the bank. I was tired of working in a hostile environment and I decided to do what was right for me. So I left Pepsi.

When I walked off that job, I was scared to death. I had no idea how I was going to make ends meet but I knew I had to get out of there before I said or did something I would later regret.

Thirty years later, I read in the newspaper that Pepsi was being sued for their hiring discrimination practices against Blacks. I wasn't surprised at all.

I was still working at the gas station but I needed another hustle. I went to work at Bob Bailey's club,

Sugarhill, which was in North Las Vegas but right next door to the Westside. I started as a bar-boy and then I became a bartender. I enjoyed the tips and I got a kick out of running into the "regular" celebrities like boxers Joe Louis and Sonny Liston, entertainer Sammy Davis Jr., and actor Greg Morris. The atmosphere was so exciting it was hard to leave, so I would stay after my shift and have a few drinks.

All work and no play was starting to make my life a little dull. I started to think about the lady I met at the car wash when I first came to Vegas. I just couldn't get her off of my mind. I looked in the phone book and asked a couple of long-time residents if they knew who she was and where would I find her. When I finally got her phone number, I called and introduced myself. Luckily, she remembered me. We started to spend quality time together and in time we grew closer which was a good thing.

Marilyn was a beautician at "Miss Elizabeth's" beauty salon on Sahara and Las Vegas Boulevard. At that time, she was probably the second Black hairdresser to work on the Strip.

One day, I walked in her shop and she introduced me to the customer in the chair. She was married to a man named Dusty, and he was the head of Burns International Security Services in Las Vegas. She thought I was the type of man he would want to have on his team and she was anxious for me to meet him.

Dusty hired me on the spot. I worked with five guys and my job was to protect the people I was assigned to and serve legal documents.

Marilyn and me

Elvis Presley was one of Burns' clients. He wanted so much to be a regular guy. He would do things like have us escort him in a 7-11 and local mom and pop stores hoping no one would notice him. On the other hand, entertainer Frank Sinatra and a few organized crime members wanted their space protected and to be discrete when they were out in public. By no means, was the job all lights, camera and action.

When I was given divorce papers to serve to a resident, I looked at the name and realized it was for a very close friend. He was a skycap at McCarran Airport and I got to know him when he and his co-workers would stop by Sugarhill after work for a drink, and when I went by his bowling alley on Jackson and C Street. There was a bar in there so we had a lot of conversations.

On the day I was scheduled to serve him the papers, I drove to his house and parked. I was nervous and anxious and completely out of my comfort zone. When I knocked on the front door, his wife answered and I became confused. I couldn't quite grasp what was going on. She told me to come in and that he was downstairs with the kids playing Monopoly.

I walked in holding the papers and man was he happy to see me. After a minute of small talk, I handed him the papers and before he realized what was going on, I made sure I was out of that house!

After that assignment, I decided working for a security firm came with a price and in the end it wouldn't be worth it. I called my friend Doug and said that I was ready to drive for the school district.

## MY FIRST BUS DRIVING JOB

I passed the bus driving test and attended orientation to learn about the dos and don'ts for kids with special needs. I knew then that working in this environment was going to make me appreciate what I have and how much I take for granted each and every day.

After I finished driving the school bus, I would go to Sugarhill and work seven to eight hour shifts. I was making a lot of money there but I was spending most of it in the bar. If I made $200 to $300 in tips a night, I would be lucky if I made it home with $50. The non-stop drinking of Seagram's VO and Coke and having to get up at 5:00 a.m. was starting to take a toll on my body. So I decided to give the gaming industry a try.

In addition to driving a bus for the school district, I went to work as a bartender in the Stardust Hotel showroom. The bar was located on the outside in the casino area and the environment was hectic and intense. You really had to have your head together there because no one wrote down the orders. They would shout them out and you better had memorized it the first time otherwise you were dinged. When I left the Stardust, I went to work for the strip club the Plush Horse. Marilyn had no problem with it. In fact, she was supportive.

Marilyn and I decided to get married. When she was pregnant with our first child, Carmen, I was happy and nervous. Being a father was a whole new world, and I knew I had to play a significant role in her life.

Every so often, when I got off work, I had to pick Carmen up at her grandmother's house which was around 1:00 a.m. Sometimes my niece, Gwen, Velma's daughter, would pick her up after she was done teaching and take her back to their house. She worked on her lesson plans and fed Carmen Hamburger Heaven French fries and that wasn't good. But Carmen thought it was great.

When Marilyn was expecting our second, Dusti, I was really messed up. I knew how to work long hours but I wasn't quite sure the kind of father I was capable of becoming. We were making a lot of money, and even though I was a focused, determined-minded man, it was nice having a lady around. She softened the blows.

Business at the beauty shop was going good. And then her boss, who was also the owner of Miss Elizabeth's, decided to retire. She wanted to hand over the shop to Marilyn, but she refused to take it. When she told me about it, I thought it was a chance of a lifetime. In those days, to own property on the Strip and be Black was unheard of and still is. For the life of me, I could not grasp where her mind was.

While I was working tirelessly to buy another house, she and her co-workers started to party on the Strip and hang out in the clubs until the wee hours of the morning.

She spent money like *water*, buying jewelry and clothes like they were necessities and claimed that it was good for business and a great way to gain customers, but I didn't see it.

I hardly slept working several jobs and now I had to deal with the fact we were going in different directions. I was bothered by it because I didn't know what to do so I chose to overlook it because I made a promise to God that I would be with this woman for the rest of my life.

My bus driving job at the Clark County School District was going as well as expected, and I was surprised when I was promoted as a Safety Director. I was responsible for developing, implementing and managing health and safety policies and procedures.

A police officer named Sergeant Rose was assigned to work with me and we both noticed an increase in students getting hit by cars when crossing the streets. We came up with a few safety measures which included providing the kids with assistance when crossing, and addressed them in front of the CCSD Board of Directors.

They were pleased with what we had to say and voted to give it a try.

Sergeant Rose and I were given names of volunteers who were willing to assist students at schools with the highest traffic flow. Even bus drivers got involved during their down time. The program was a success. Crosswalk and Pedestrian laws were established and traffic control speed limits were set. And when the Metropolitan Police Department found funding to pay the volunteers, we made sure schools practiced adequate safety measures when crossing the street. **That is how the Crosswalk Guard position started in Clark County, and the founders were Sergeant Rose and me.**

Working as a bartender as one of my side gigs was cool, but after my shift I enjoyed it even more by indulging in a few too many. I needed to feel safe to have a more solid foundation and the only way to achieve that was to be my own boss. As much as I hated to admit it, it was time for another change, and just like the other positions had proven in the past, I was confident things were going to fall in place.

# CHAPTER FIVE
# THE WHEELS OF CHANGE

In 1973, I left the school district to work as a bus driver for Transportation Unlimited (TUI) which had around 30 commercial buses. Starting at 5:00 a.m., I would pick up workers from various points and transport them to the Nevada Test Site by 7:30 a.m. The drivers had a choice to stay in a small hotel until 2:00 p.m. or park their bus and ride back on one that was headed back to Las Vegas and stay until it was time to go back up to the Test Site to take the workers to their drop off points.

Since 1951, the Nevada Test Site was one of the most significant weapons sites in the United States, where nuclear testing, both atmospheric and underground, took place.

When I left the district, I withdrew my monies from my PERS (Public Employees' Retirement System) account and purchased an Eagle bus. I had been thinking seriously about getting into the transportation business for quite some time, so I decided to act on my impulse, only to find out I would need a whole bunch of licenses to get started.

The first bus I bought was an Eagle.
It broke down more than it was in service.

In addition to my job at TUI, I began driving on the weekends for a private club called Bob Spencer's Travel Club. I made short trips to popular spots like Knott's Berry Farm, Disneyland, and various tourist attractions in Southern California. Every Saturday, I would drive a group of people to St. George, Utah just so they could worship all day.

I transported the Bishop Gorman High School football team to and from games, and the students at Nellis Air Force Base to St. Christopher's Catholic School and Bishop Gorman High School. I also drove a van for the Church of Jesus Christ of Latter-day Saints to transport girls in the system to their group home.

After Marilyn walked away from the opportunity to own her own beauty shop, she went to work for a guy named Jerry, the owner of a shop in the Aladdin Hotel. We bought a home on Jones and Charleston and then we bought another one in Summerlin around Rainbow and Sahara.

We tried counseling but it didn't work; our viewpoints had become way too different. She believed in investing in jewelry and I trusted my money in property and this didn't help matters between us. And since our first daughter Carmen was in college and our second, Dusti, was in high school, we decided this would be the perfect time to go our separate ways. She kept the two houses and I moved back in the one on Brady. I was back where I started from.

Although we were only separated, I felt for the first time in my life that I had failed. And I knew when I agreed to call it quits it was going to be something I would regret for the rest of my life.

I was finally making enough money to quit my job at the Plush Horse and concentrate on the transportation world. But I still needed to figure out how to start my own business and get the licenses needed to move my bus from the front of my house and on the road. Then out of the blue, my friend Doug called and said he and a few other people wanted to use my bus for upcoming events.

In those days, Nevada lacked public transportation and the only two bus companies were LTR (**L**as Vegas-**T**onopah-**R**eno) Stage Lines and Gray Line Tours, which was used for sightseeing tours. But because Las Vegas was growing at a rapid pace, transportation was becoming a major concern.

I met with my life-long friends: Bob Conner, James Ray Enus, and Douglas Ray McCain to discuss the possibility of developing our own bus company. Bob was not interested, so we thought the name of the company should be Triple R Enterprises after our middle initials. Then James said he wanted to go back to school to get an engineering degree which left Doug and me. We decided to name the company Ray & Ross Transport Inc., our middle names with me being the Ross. We were contracted to transport the kids at Nellis, and the construction workers at the Test Site paid on an individual basis.

In 1975, when TUI lost the Nevada Test Site contract, it was granted back to LTR. At this time, the federal government paid to transport the white collar workers but left the several thousands of construction workers, who were mostly Black, to get to work on their own.

The construction workers would begin their drive to the Test Site at 3:00 a.m., work 8 to 10 hours, drive back and stop by a nearby bar. There were so many accidents along the highway they nicknamed it "The Widow Maker." The government became aware that they excluded the workers and decided to allow all employees the opportunity to ride the buses. And that's when we informed them we were available.

When we applied for a charter and sight-seeing bus license, we were rejected three times by the Public Service Commission because we didn't meet the financial and mechanical standards. Once we corrected what was missing, we reapplied but were rejected a fourth time.

Chelsea Morgan and my Ray & Ross partner Douglas Ray McCain at a company fundraiser at Cashman Field

The Public Service Certificate went to Westside Charter, a Black-owned bus line, instead of us, but they did not have a license for sight-seeing. Westside Charter was owned by Lonnie Chaney and his business partner but Arthur "Art" Chapman was the brains behind the company. Art was the designer of McCarran Airport's transportation system.

I had a good relationship with TUI's owners, Rosemary Pitch and her husband Tony, but when I found out they were in the middle of a divorce, I was curious about the company. They were in and out of court. At first she was awarded the company then it went to him and then back to her.

I decided to sit down and talk to them about an asking price for their license. The three of us agreed on $60,000 only to find out later that we couldn't buy a license because the law didn't allow it. They decided to sell the company to us on credit with the stipulation that we pay a certain amount each month. So in addition to the license, we inherited 30 buses but we only kept two because equipment was sold off some of them and the others were not in working condition.

Transportation Unlimited owner Rosemary Pitch

# RAY & ROSS

Ray & Ross Transport, Inc. was starting to show potential. We bought a few buses and parked them on a vacant lot on H Street and Owens Avenue where a car wash was once located. Eventually, we leased an old tri-plex located next to Ewing Brothers Towing on A Street.

We remodeled the inside for offices and built a shop out back. In 1981, we bought 15 acres of land on the corner of D Street and Owens Avenue, which later became 300 West Owens.

Ray & Ross Transport, Inc. was located near
D Street and Owens Avenue.

The foundation was concrete because a hotel was planned but never built. It was said that singer and pianist, Dinah Washington was behind the project but for some reason it fell through.

The Nevada Department of Transportation was repaving the streets on the Westside and when we asked the supervisor if they could dump the excess dirt on our lot, he had no problem with it. There must have been eight feet poured which flattened the surface and evened it out perfectly. Now we were in a position to add a garage and hire a mechanic.

We built a 4000 square foot building which housed the offices in front and a shop in the back, hired more professional office support and created a Sales Department. Susan Pence and Victoria Monroe eventually had everything running smoothly in the offices. Soon after, our first Sales Manager, Jackie Brady would come on board.

A few years later, when I returned to my hometown of Camden, my brother Willie's daughter Trish came back with me to work for Ray & Ross. Shortly after, her sister Cynthia decided to join the team.

We had three buses we were using to transport the Test Site construction workers and the kids at Nellis. But in 1981, there was a fuel shortage in the country and the feds decided all Nevada Test Site workers could ride the LTR buses, which would have put us out of business.

My friend George Sherman was a former Tuskegee Airman and a contract administrator for R.E.E.C.O. (Reynolds Electric & Engineering Company) the corporation that managed personnel, operations, maintenance and administration at the Nevada Test Site. When I called to tell him what happened, he suggested I meet him to discuss my options.

My friend and Driver Supervisor, Elgin Simpson and I met George at a bar and he didn't waste any time with his advice. Without directly saying it, he made sure we knew we needed to look into the federal laws about the government competing with privately owned companies. He knew it was in there, he just wanted us to find it.

After thorough research, sure enough we found the law that restricts the federal government from ignoring the existence of a private industry and immediately submitted it to them. The contract that was granted to LTR now included Ray & Ross.

We were issued a contract for our three buses to transport workers at the Test Site, and a few months later we were granted another contract to operate three more buses. But we didn't have them.

I was fully aware that the Greyhound Lines would run their GMC buses for 10 to 12 years then sell them. When I asked the owner Dick Seitzinger about them, he agreed to sell us four. I added an extra bus in case one broke down.

The style and mechanisms were starting to change and we needed to update our fleet. We started off with a GMC bus model 4106 but the company went out of business because of the constant problems they were having with the transmission. While traveling downhill, the gears had to be shifted correctly otherwise you may never be able to shift back. During this time the brakes would heat up and stop working properly. They worked at certain times of the summer but for the most part they would overheat, and the engine was not designed for a bus. On top of that, it only held a maximum of 32 passengers.

So, we stopped using the GMC buses and replaced them with the MCI model. It had a standard shift and was much easier to operate and could hold 47 passengers. It was built in Canada but before it was shipped, the tires and bumpers were removed. But as soon as it landed in the states, the parts were installed and it was labeled "Made in the USA".

In 1985, I was recognized by the State of Nevada as the Minority Small Business Person of the Year. Ray & Ross was finally starting to roll.

Minority Small Business Person of the Year award

# CHAPTER SIX
# WE ROLLIN NOW

L ong before we began transporting employees to and from the Nevada Test Site, we ran Interstate Charter Buses, and still continued to do so. One of our favorite charter customers was Skinny Dugan's Bar & Grill. Owners Bobby and Freddy Keck sponsored a softball team and we took them to their away games in various parts of California and Utah. Their restaurant was our 'off-premises conference room'. We worked out a lot of important business there and enjoyed a lot of hot wings as well.

In those days, at the 'old' Alamo Airport on Las Vegas Boulevard, the buses were allowed right on the tarmac and were able to park alongside the airplanes. It would later be bought by Howard Hughes and re-named McCarran.

I will never forget the day I was scheduled to transport President Bill Clinton, his staff, and a few members from the media. I parked as close as I could and the moment he stepped off the plane I greeted him. It was a surreal moment, and truly unforgettable.

I worked on Clinton's campaign in 1997, and afterwards I provided Secretary of Transportation Rodney Slater information about the disproportionate number of Blacks in transportation and as vendors in airports across the nation, specifically at McCarran.

One day, I picked up the phone and Clinton's voice was on the other end. He appreciated my ideas on how to get more Blacks out to vote, about the Welfare-to-Work programs, and the upward mobility for Blacks in the job market. He was fully aware of the discrepancies Blacks faced, many of them a direct result of decisions made by Republican legislators. They prefer to mail in their ballots but sometimes the mail service was not reliable.

President Bill Clinton arrives at McCarran Airport

To receive a phone call from President Clinton
was a surreal moment

In time, Ray & Ross became the official bus company for Bishop Gorman High School and the University of Nevada, Las Vegas (UNLV). We transported their sports teams to and from the airport. When UNLV played Hawaii in a bowl tournament, we utilized 30 buses to transport the people who were in town for the event.

We also provided transportation for the Clark County School District (CCSD) football teams. We made several trips to St. George, Utah for Bonanza High School, but I wasn't quite sure what that connection was all about. We were growing and we needed more buses.

I met with the executive director of the Small Business Administration (SBA) to enquire about getting another loan. My friend Art Williams, the attorney and Chief Legal Counsel for REECO, and his boss Ed Weintraub, came with me. I asked for a $500,000 advance, but the manager at Nevada State Bank told him I could be approved for $1 million. I started to sing to myself the lyrics of Stevie Wonder's Martin Luther King Jr. birthday song: "Happy birthday to you, Happy Birrrrrthday..."

We decided to buy our next buses from a Canadian company. When I made plans to go to Canada, the Test Site arranged for their chief mechanic, Joe Booze to accompany me to inspect the buses. I ended up buying eight. I drove one back to Las Vegas and the others were driven by seven of my drivers. The owner of the bus company in Canada wanted his son to come back with me. He became my garage foreman and with my help he has been here ever since.

Small Business Award
L: Senator James Bilbray and Senator Dick Gephardt

In 1988, we were awarded the larger Nevada Test Site contract and we were in need of more space. We bought eight more buses, and added a 10,000 square foot enclosed bus maintenance garage and state-of-the-art bus washing and detailing facility on the property. We built a block wall around the entire property and secured it with electronic gates.

After Ray & Ross' place of business was established, I bought the nearby property located on the corner of D Street (1601). It was a Mobile gas station owned by Tolefree Towing. I rented it to Doug Gibson, who continues to operate his business, Doug's Automotive Electronic Emissions today.

Doug Gibson served in the United States Air Force for 23 years and will forever be a legend in his field. He was the First Black Crew Chief with the air demonstration squadron "Thunderbirds" and a Production Supervisor for the Air Force Fighter Weapons School.

By 1989, Ray & Ross had a total of 36 buses. Our contract with the Nevada Test Site paid 99% of our employees' salaries and 90% of our bus maintenance costs.

When we bought TUI, Jim Kaufield, former Operations Manager at TUI, had come on board and developed our Operations Department from the ground up.

Elgin Simpson, our Driver Supervisor, was now managing 65 drivers. Jim had all the Operations experience we needed for as big as we were getting, and for developing our airport mini-bus side of the business. We added 15 mini-buses for international junkets at the airport. Our job was to pick up the tourists the second they stepped off the airplane and immediately take them to their hotel. When a title fight was scheduled, we were assigned designated guests to pick up and ensure that they got to their correct hotels.

One of my favorite memories is of all the fun our kids had working as On Call Tour Coordinators. My daughter Dusti and Susan's son Greg would go with the buses and meet the incoming international flights. They had their hands full, gathering up excited tourists and getting them to the buses without letting them stray into the long banks of airport slot machines.

Governor List was in office at the time and Nevada had a lot of federal funding floating around. I heard about a contract called the Mail-Run. It only had two stops in town, the Wyandotte Building (the downtown administration building for REECO) and the Department of Energy (DOE).

Ray & Ross Sales Manager Jackie Brady and my former real estate agent and NEEDCO founder,
Dr. William "Bob" Bailey

Pictures of about ninety percent of
Ray & Ross drivers (above) and staff

It did not require a special license so we applied and landed it. But then political powers stepped in and gave it to Westside Charter. They utilized it for three years, then it was granted back to us.

Switching our contract to Westside Charter was a political move and key employees who worked at the Public Service Commission were tired of being in the middle of the bull. The chairman quit and went back to Washington D.C. as well as three of the attorneys.

At that time, Ray & Ross was the largest Black owned business in Nevada. It had grown into a multimillion dollar enterprise that employed more than 160 people and we deliberately focused on the unemployable and non-minority people who, in many cases, were considered unemployable, due to the lack of skills or a blemish on their record.

# CHAPTER SEVEN
## POWER OF GIVING

N ow that I was in a position to have received so much, the gift at this point was to give back. I believe that there could be no definition of success if it did not include the service to others. So when the Rodney King "race" Riot broke out in Los Angeles on April 29, 1992, I saw an opportunity to offer my assistance.

The riot created disorder and complete confusion on the Westside, and the residents rebelled by destroying buildings which caused certain areas to be without power, telephone, gas, and water. The damages from this riot were much worse than those from the Watts Riot.

I wanted to help. So on the corner of H and Owens, I organized the representatives from the utilities and Metro police department to walk around and find out which residents in the area needed restoration. I told my friends to fire up the barbeque pits and I supplied food and water for everyone involved. It was a successful collaborative effort.

This riot created disturbances all over the world for five whole days, injuring innocent people. It was a reaction from the acquittal of four police officers for severely beating Rodney King, a Black man, regardless of the direct evidence of a videotape of the incident that was aired on just about every broadcast station in the country.

What was also troubling about the Riot was that a lot of hard working people lost their livelihoods. And once again, Nucleus Plaza (aka Golden West) which was very much needed in the community, was practically destroyed.

Representatives from the utilities and police departments
came together to help restore the Westside
after the Rodney King Riot

I started to sponsor sporting events, and host special programs that would benefit our youth. I was an avid contributor to the University of Nevada, Las Vegas (UNLV) Rebels, and I made time to recruit assistance at the campus as well.

NBA Players. L-R: Muggsy Bogues, Mark Jackson, Dominique Wilkins, Sidney Green, and Reggie Theus

L-R: Jim Kaufield, our Operations Manager in the background, Las Vegas Convention and Visitors Authority President/CEO Rossi Ralenkotter, and Thomas & Mack Director Dennis Finfrock

Former football player, coach, and analyst Lou Holtz

L-R: Mr. Finley, NFL players Raymond Chester
and Jack Tatum

And of course, I couldn't resist participating in the Martin Luther King Parade. The event took place downtown on Fremont Street, and I made sure that one of our buses, which was the first "articulated" bus owned and operated in Las Vegas, was decorated and the colors expressed how grateful we were to everyone who contributed to our success.

I made sure the first "articulated" bus owned and operated in Las Vegas participated in the Martin Luther King Jr. Parade on Fremont Street

# LAS VEGAS
# PUBLIC HOUSING AUTHORITY

In 1991, I was appointed on the Board of the Las Vegas Public Housing Authority by the first female Mayor of Las Vegas, Jan Jones Blackhurst. I was then voted to be the Vice Chair, and Louis Connor, the owner of Seven Seas Restaurant, served as President.

Jan Jones Blackhurst, the first woman to serve as Mayor of Las Vegas, appointed me to the Board of the Las Vegas Public Housing Authority

Although there were several highlights I can vividly recall, one in particular was when several of us on the Board went to Washington, D.C. to meet with the Secretary of Housing and Urban Development (HUD), Jack Kemp (1989-1993). An Executive Order to integrate all public housing had just been signed by President George H. W. Bush, and we were there to give him our perspectives on how to implement the particulars. Shortly after our visit, Secretary Kemp toured potential public housing areas in Las Vegas.

Jack Kemp was a Private in the U.S. Army and served from 1958-1962. He played the quarterback position for various NFL teams (1957-1969), but what I remember most about him is his direct and bold speeches. I recall one in particular, and I loved it when he said:

> *Pro football gave me a good perspective. When I entered the political arena, I had already been booed, cheered, cut, sold, traded, and hung in effigy.*

Around this time, former world No. 1 tennis player and Las Vegas born, Andre Agassi wanted to build a Boys

& Girls Club and a private secondary school in a predominately Black Community often referred to as the "Historic Westside". Working with the Andre Agassi Foundation for Education and the Boys & Girls Clubs of America, we identified that the perfect location for the project would be the A. D. Guy Center, which was named after Addeliar D. Guy III, the first Black judge on the state court bench in Nevada.

The building, owned by the City of Las Vegas, was housing off-campus classes for the Clark County Community College, but had become outdated and dilapidated. We negotiated with the City to demolish the old and rebuild a brand new one that would suitably house both the Boys & Girls Club and the Community College classes. Since our plans for the facility exceeded this one property, we negotiated with the Las Vegas Public Housing Authority and HUD to obtain adjoining land so we could build Mr. Agassi's dream and still continue to provide plenty of room for the Community College classes. He required that the plans include tennis courts, so the basketball courts were replaced.

The Dr. Martin Luther King Committee was holding their meetings at the Guy center, and there was no room for them in the planned Agassi building. So we negotiated with HUD for office space across the street for them.

During this time, we were also negotiating to obtain land for the Andre Agassi College Preparatory Academy. We met with the City of Las Vegas to inquire about the land they owned, and to purchase some private houses at market value. These thorough discussions eventually resulted in the first and only private charter school in the history of the Westside that provided a first-class K-12 education that prepared them for an extensive education.

In 2017, Agassi Prep decided to turn over operations to Democracy Prep after successfully graduating 9 senior classes. But even so, I will always hold the highest regards for Mr. Agassi for remembering the kids in the community. He has been a great influence and more importantly, he showed the public that it could be done and that they matter.

Soon after the Agassi projects were completed, we were informed that neither the City of North Las Vegas nor the City of Henderson had Boys & Girls Clubs. So after working with the Boys & Girls Clubs of America, we purchased an abandoned fire station the City of NLV owned, remodeled and customized it and launched the new Boys and Girls Club. We made the same arrangements for the City of Henderson. Today, all the Clubs are open and successfully providing for the kids in the community.

# BUSINESS VENTURES

Not that my plate was not full enough, I started to invest in various businesses to build a stronger financial portfolio.

Armstrong Cellular was located in the Armstrong's Travel office. The first year we were in business, it was very profitable. But then all the major companies began to take an interest in cellular phones and the little businesses like mine were squeezed out.

A young lady named Alisha Bell managed this enterprise until the day we closed. She was working on a master's degree in education at the University of Nevada, Las Vegas and after completing her courses, she moved to

Detroit where she became involved in politics. Today, she is the County Commissioner Chair of Wayne County and is in her 9th 2-year term. She represents District 7, which includes neighborhoods in central and western Detroit.

Senator Harry Reid and Wayne County Commission Chair Alisha Bell. She used to manage my cellular company

Aubrey Branch owned a life insurance office in North Las Vegas. He was struggling so I helped him financially and also served on his advisory board. As his business grew, he relocated from Decatur and Carey and opened his full service Branch Insurance Agency on the corner of Smoke Ranch Road and Decatur Boulevard, which is still in operation today as the Branch and Hernandez Agency.

In 1998, I purchased the land the old Johnson Supermarket was located on (1200 N. D Street). The Fresh Start Baptist Church had been renting a building located on H Street, but to their surprise, their landlord decided to sell the property, and the church couldn't afford to buy it. My former Ray & Ross Parts Manager, Alphonso Eason introduced me to the minister of the church, Pastor Ezra Bell because he was fully aware that I was the owner of that property. I had the building renovated for them to lease and they've been there ever since.

For many years, Ezra Bell was a mechanic at the Nevada Test Site and then he went to work for the Las Vegas Transit System. His wife, First Lady Fannie Bell, was a Senior Staff Attendant at the Nevada Test Site.

When a few of my friends approached me about an investment opportunity, I had to hear what they had to say. Apparently, they started the construction of a convenience store on W. Owens Avenue, but had run out of funds and needed an investor. I saw it as a great business opportunity so I moved on it. The store opened and showed potential for about two years, but then due to poor management, we had no choice but to sell it. The next owners failed as well, and it sat vacant for many years. Then Terrible Herbst Corporation came in and purchased it, and today, a fully operating store and a Chevron gas station exist.

One day, while driving down Las Vegas Boulevard, I noticed an old run-down building that had a liquor store in the front and a car rental agency in the back. It was located across the street from the Hacienda Hotel, which is now Mandalay Bay Resorts. I called my real estate agent, Bonnie Juniel and asked if she would check into it.

She said it was in foreclosure and the owner was a Jewish man who lived in San Francisco. I arranged for her to fly out to meet with him and over dinner, they negotiated a deal. He offered to sell it for $30,000 and I told her to go with it.

The building was in need of some serious reconstruction. I removed the debris from the inside then I had it demolished. I moved a Ray & Ross trailer, which was more like a mobile home, on the premises to serve as an office for us and the official place to stage tours for our buses.

I then established a loan out of San Bernardino, California, and hired the architect Mel Green and contractor Lou Richardson to design and rebuild the property. When we came to an agreement on how it should look, they submitted the plans to the Clark County Building Department for approval. For one entire year, we did not hear one word about our plans. I called Senator Harry Reid and told him about the delay, and he also thought it was very unusual. Three months later, he called my office and said that my plans were approved and ready to be picked up.

In December of 2021, I was so pleased when McCarran Airport was renamed after Harry Reid, and that the ceremony took place a few weeks before he passed. Not only was he the longest-serving U.S. Senator in Nevada history, he helped to secure millions for the completion of the airport. Harry was a great man who served as President Obama's Majority Leader. On the other hand, Senator Pat McCarran had a history of perpetuating racism, xenophobia and antisemitism.

My strip mall, "Mr. A's Plaza" was finally complete and ready to be leased. My real estate agent, a Black lady whose name I can't recall, was in charge of getting the building occupied. She said that people would call to set up an appointment, and after a quick tour, they would leave and not call back to discuss any details. I never got anyone to move into my place; it turned out to be a bad investment.

To my knowledge, there is not one Black person who owns a business on the Las Vegas Strip. Back then it was unheard of.

I never thought this would happen to such a nice building that was in a prime location. This wasn't the first time I heard of this sort of thing happening to one of us.

Even the top brass experienced racist mistreatments for having an investment on the Strip.

When famed entertainer, Sammy Davis Jr. owned shares in a hotel, he was forced to relinquish his interest. And when Dr. James McMillan, Nevada's first Black dentist and former Las Vegas NAACP president, owned shares in a major Strip hotel, he never received a cent for them. One day, when he went to a board meeting, he was asked why he was there. He then found out that his name had been removed from all documents and was never given an explanation.

Mr. A's Plaza on Las Vegas Boulevard

Then I got a notice about my sign. The County claimed that the building was the required 50 feet or more off the Strip (the street) but because the sign was too big, it did not meet the zoning regulations.

Representatives of Jack In The Box were interested in building in front of my mall. We negotiated a 30 year lease and two 30 year options, which was a total of 90 years. When the paperwork was completed, I got a call to attend a meeting at a real estate agency. The president was flying in from Phoenix, Arizona and when he finally arrived, he sat down and introduced himself. Then his cell phone rang. He stepped out to take the call and said he would be back in 30 minutes. I haven't seen him since.

I was paying $16,000 a month on my loan for the strip mall and I only had two renters. The guy who owned the rental car agency lived in Reno. When his wife called and said he died and that she was closing the agency that left the liquor store. And then they closed. Suddenly, I had zero income. To save the mall, I went to court and filed bankruptcy.

The Hacienda Hotel was in the process of selling to Mandalay Bay Resorts. This would mean that when you exit the hotel, you would come straight across the street to my property. But then I found out that the Mandalay Bay's new entrance was moved further down, and from there my building was nowhere to be seen.

Needless to say, I was spending a whole lot of time at Seven Seas, a club on the Westside. While sitting at the bar in my usual seat, I got a call from the owner of "Flying J" truck stop which was one of his many properties. He was interested in purchasing my mall.

When we met to work out the particulars, he told me that he represented a hotel chain out of France and they were trying to buy that entire area, which included a McDonalds, a liquor store, a Buster Brown shoe store, and a coffee shop. He made me an offer I couldn't refuse and boy was that a relief.

The last time I went by my used-to-be mall, it was vacant. I still don't understand how that could be.

# CHAPTER EIGHT
## THIS IS YOUR LIFE

On March 4, 1989, the Beta Eta Theta Chapter of Gamma Phi Delta Sorority honored me with a "This is Your Life, Sam Armstrong" celebration at Bally's Grand Hotel. I was informed about it a month ahead of time and since it was a fundraising event for the Sorority, I helped to promote it. It was an amazing experience, one I will always cherish, and the speeches, letters, and words expressed by my friends and acquaintances were so surreal, even I was convinced that I wasn't such a bad guy.

My close friend and life-long advisor, Bob Connor attended and gave the following speech.

*Sam and I have had a long and rewarding relationship. But the most interesting portion of that friendship developed during the formation and building of his bus company, which is presently known as Ray & Ross Transport. He started with an older model Eagle bus. That's something important to Sam. He was so proud of it. When it wasn't in use, we used to go cruise in it... There is no thrill like no ride in that 46 foot bus-40 foot long with the engine doors propped open back there.*

*Anyway, Sam was very optimistic about being in business, and as always, you do anything you can to help a friend with his new business. I remember once he needed fuel for the bus for a charter and didn't have money. I charged the fuel on my Chevron credit card. Bill came in and my wife asked me, "Where on earth did you go and what were you driving?! There are 144 gallons of gas on here!"*

*Anyway, as I said, Sam was optimistic. In the early years of his business, I found myself staying at home a lot, much the same way parents do when their daughter's out on a date and you wonder when she's going to get home. With the equipment that Sam had at that time, it meant he could break down anywhere, at any time. And because he was a one-man operation, we were his dispatchers-all of his friends were on call. Whoever answered the phone had to go and get him and offer Sam help.*

*So Sam, I'd like to say thanks for becoming a success and getting me out of the dispatcher business.*

*Sam Armstrong has the ability to extract the very best from all of his family, friends, colleagues and anybody else he was around. And with that I learned a lot about myself and the fact that I had a lot of hidden talents. I learned how to change air bags on a leased diesel bus before I learned how to install a set of shocks on my own car. I learned how to build a prototype air conditioner from a few bus air conditioner parts and a swamp cooler.*

*I also learned that you may have to go to several 24-hour grocery stores at night, but that you can find enough motor oil to fill the engine of a bus at 1 a.m. in the morning. I also learned that it takes $20 in quarters at a 25¢ car wash to wash a 40-foot bus inside and out. And that after washing we'd have to drive it up on cinder blocks slanted to the right so the water would drain out.*

*I learned that it takes 145 cans of spray paint, four people and a day-and-a-half to paint a 40-foot bus in an open-air environment. I also learned that a Chevrolet Monte Carlo tape deck can be installed in an Eagle bus and it will sound great if you have the right kind of speakers.*

*Sam was ingenious at keeping that one bus running, inventing parts, doing whatever. If he hadn't been successful in the transportation business he might very well have been a world class inventor.*

*But most of all, I learned from Sam that you can succeed against all odds if you truly believe in what you are doing. Sam, thank you for the things I've learned from you. I wish you good health, good luck and continued success.*

My lifetime friend Bob Conner speaking at the event

My close friend James Enus spoke about the time I was determined to invent a vehicle that could carry my tools and other things I found myself toting around 24/7.

*A few years ago, my good friend became very restless, as he often does, and decided that he needed a carry-all type of automobile. So he went searching. Sam found himself a $150 Jeep Wagoneer. The only problem was the rear end was all rusted out. That wouldn't do. So Sam went out searching, and lo and behold, Sam found another $150 Jeep Wagoneer. This one had the front end all crushed in. That wouldn't do either. Next thing I knew, Sam had bought both the $150 Jeep Wagoneers, cut them in half, and welded the two good ends together. But Sam still wasn't happy with his now $300 Jeep.*

*I was in the stereo business at the time. He came to me and said, "I want music in my car."*
*I said, "Sam, I've got a nice $75 AM/FM stereo cassette radio for your $300 Jeep."*

*He said, "No, I have a dream..." So we proceeded to install a $2,000 stereo system in his $300 Jeep.*

*Sam still wasn't happy. Sam put in carpet. He painted. He soundproofed. In other words, he perfected his Jeep Wagoneer. When there was nothing else possible to be done with the Jeep;*

*when there was no more challenge; when there was no more dream ... Sam sold the Jeep.*

*What I got from all this was: Sam is a Dreamer. Sam will work very hard to make his dreams come true. Ray & Ross is a testament to his willingness to work to make a dream come true. I call him a Dreamer. I also call him my Friend. Congratulations, Sam.*

My lifetime friend James Enus

My friend Louis McGhee read a deeply sentimental poem by Edgar Guest also known as "the poet of the people." It was entitled "It Couldn't Be Done."

*Somebody said that it couldn't be done, but he with a chuckle replied that "maybe it couldn't," but he would be one who wouldn't say so till he'd tried. So he buckled right in with the trace of a grin on his face. If he worried he hid it. He started to sing as he tackled the thing that couldn't be done, and he did it.*

My lifetime friend Louis McGhee

My Brother Billie was the only sibling who was able to attend the event. I was happy that he was there to share the evening with me. I really enjoyed what he had to say.

My brother Billie Armstrong

United States Senator of Nevada Richard Bryan attended. And he said something I will never forget.

*I see Sammie at all these different events. He always has a smile on his face, but I also see that he'd probably rather be watching football with his friends than getting all dressed up and attending these functions. He's here because he knows it's necessary to promote his business.*

United States Senator Richard Bryan

The Senator's Liaison, Brenda Williams was also in attendance. She is a very good friend and today we make it a point to check on each other on a regular basis.

For all those who were unable to attend, a letter was presented to me by a member of their staff. United States Senator of Nevada Harry Reid was unable to attend, but instead he sent his Community Liaison Eric Jordan to present a letter.

With United States Senator Harry Reid at a fundraising event

HARRY REID
NEVADA

COMMITTEES:
APPROPRIATIONS
ENVIRONMENT AND PUBLIC WORKS
SPECIAL COMMITTEE ON AGING

## United States Senate
WASHINGTON, DC 20510

March 3, 1989

Gamma Phi Delta Sorority, Inc.
Beta Eta Theta Chapter
Bally's Grand Hotel
Las Vegas, Nevada

Dear Ladies:

Thank you for your invitation to attend your Sixth Annual "This is Your Life" Banquet. Please accept my warmest congratulations to your organization for its continuing effort to raise funds for the higher education of our youth. It was Mary McLeod Bethune who noted some fifty years ago, "Knowledge is the prime need of the hour." That is especially true today. Your dedication and contribution to the acquisition of knowledge and education is truly commendable.

To the Honoree, my friend Sammie Armstrong, I extend my heartiest congratulations. Your recognition tonight is well deserved, and it reinforces our community's appreciation of your commitment of time, energy and resources. You are a beacon of light for others to be guided by.

Again, I applaud you all, and pledge all my support.

Sincerely,

HARRY REID
United States Senator

HMR/mr

CARSON CITY
600 E. WILLIAMS ST., SUITE 302
CARSON CITY, NV 88701
(702) 882-7343

LAS VEGAS
701 E. BRIDGER ST., SUITE 700
LAS VEGAS, NV 89101
(702) 388-6545

RENO
300 BOOTH ST.
RENO, NV 89509
(702) 784-5568

WASHINGTON, DC
U.S. SENATE
WASHINGTON, DC 20510
(202) 224-3542

United States Senator Harry Reid

UNIVERSITY OF NEVADA, LAS VEGAS
Office of the President
4505 Maryland Parkway
Las Vegas, Nevada 89154
(702) 739-3201


February 7, 1989


Mrs. Sarann Knight-Preddy, Chairperson
This is Your Life Banquet
Beta Eta Theta Chapter,
 Gamma Phi Delta Sorority
Post Office Box 4122
Las Vegas, Nevada 89127

Dear Mrs. Knight-Preddy:

Thank you very much for your kind invitation to attend the Sixth
Annual "This is Your Life" banquet on March 4 at Bally's Grand
Hotel.  There is nothing I would enjoy more--indeed, I have
attended every such banquet you've invited me to since I've been
in Las Vegas--but unfortunately I have a prior commitment, of
long standing, which will prevent my being with you this year.

I do hope you will let Mr. Armstrong know that only a conflict of
the kind I have would keep me from being present to tell the
group assembled what a great guy I think he is.

Have another great banquet this year!

Warm personal regards.

                          Sincerely,

                          Robert C. Maxson
                          President

RCM:msw

Enclosure

President of UNLV Robert Maxson

National Forum for Black Public Administrators

1301 Pennsylvania Avenue, NW
Washington, DC 20004
(202) 626-4900

February 17, 1989

**Officers**

Henry Gardner
*President*

Jack Bond
*1st Vice President*

Daniel Boggan, Jr.
*2nd Vice President*

Corene Collins
*Secretary/Treasurer*

**Board of Directors**

Randall C. Bacon
Benjamin Blakney
Walter D. Broadnax
Andrew W. Cameron
Terry Childers
Marcia L. Conner
Cynthia Curry
Carole Dortch
Don T. Dudley
James L. Francis
Sharon Gist Gilliam
Angela Hughes
Richard Knight, Jr.
Fred Martin
Richard A. Monteilh
David E. Rivers
Valerie Rivers
Carol B. Thompson
John Touchstone
Toni-Michelle Travis
Regina V. K. Williams

**Executive Advisor
to the Board**

Maynard Jackson

**Legal Counsel**

Robert Washington, Jr.

**Executive Director**

Quentin R. Lawson

Mr. Sammie R. Armstrong
President/General Manager
Ray & Ross Transport, Inc.
300 W. Owens Avenue
Las Vegas, NV 89106

Dear Sammie:

I sincerely regret that I will not be able to attend the sixth annual "This Is Your Life" banquet on Saturday March 4th. Other commitments prevent me from attending this most auspicious event. However, I cannot think of anyone more deserving of this honor than yourself.

I join the Gamma Phi Delta Sorority, Inc., Beta Eta Theta Chapter in paying tribute to you. I commend the women of Gamma Phi Delta in making an excellent selection by choosing you as their honoree. They truly selected an "outstanding" person for this honor.

I am deeply grateful for your continuing support of the National Forum for Black Public Administrators. Ever since learning about the organization, you have been extremely supportive of us. The growth and development of NFBPA is due in part to your unselfish giving of yourself to aid the organization. We are extremely proud to see one of our members receiving this honor.

Once again, my heartfelt congratulations to you on receiving this honor. It is indeed a pity that I will not be able to be in Las Vegas to share in this night of honor. My best wishes to you and keep up the good work.

Sincerely,

Quentin R. Lawson
Executive Director

The National Forum for Black Public Administrators

WILLIAM U. PEARSON
Commissioner

*Board of County Commissioners*

CLARK COUNTY BRIDGER BUILDING
225 BRIDGER AVENUE
LAS VEGAS, NEVADA 89155
(702) 455-3500

March 2, 1989

Mr. Sammie Ross Armstrong
President
Ray & Ross Transport, Inc.
300 W. Owens Avenue
Las Vegas, Nevada  89106

Dear Sam:

It is with a distinct pleasure and a great sense of pride that I
congratulate you on your selection to be the honoree of the "This
Is Your Life" banquet.

I have always been impressed with your ability to succeed in a
business where others have failed.  Your persistence in doing all
of the things that are commensurate with success is well known and
highly respected.

I regret that I will be unable to attend the affair due to prior
commitments, but I wanted to take this opportunity to personally
commend you on your unselfish contributions to this community.

AGAIN, CONGRATULATIONS!!!!

Sincerely,

DR. W. U. PEARSON
County Commissioner

WP/fl

Commissioner Dr. William U. Pearson

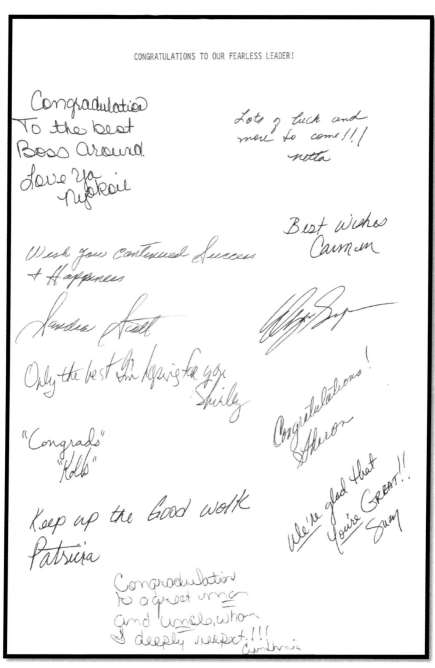

CONGRATULATIONS TO OUR FEARLESS LEADER!

Congratulations To the best Boss Around. Love Ya Nykoie

Lots of luck and more to come!!! netta

Wish you continued Success + Happiness

Sandra Scott

Best wishes Carmen

Only the best I'm hoping for you Shirley

"Congrads" "Kolb"

Congratulations! Sheron

Keep up the Good work Patricia

We're glad that you're GREAT!! Sam

Congratulations to a great man and uncle, whom I deeply respect!!! Cynthia

Congratulatory sheet signed by Ray & Ross employees

# Local businessman to be honored at sorority dinner

Gamma Phi Delta Sorority (Beta Eta Theta chapter), a national business and professional women's organization, will present its eighth annual "This Is Your Life" banquet Saturday at Bally's.

This year's event will honor Sammie Ross Armstrong, president and general manager of Ray & Ross Transport Inc.

The gala event will highlight Armstrong's life from childhood years through his business accomplishments.

Proceeds from this year's dinner will benefit the sorority's "scholarship fund," with this year's special scholarship being presented in honor of Arm-

**S.R. ARMSTRONG**

strong.

For further information regarding the banquet and no-host cocktails, call Sarah Ann Knight Preddy, chairwoman, at 648-5040.

# Former Camdenite to be honored

LAS VEGAS — Sammie Ross Armstrong, formerly of Camden and the son of the late George and Annie Armstrong, will be honored March 4 by the Beta Eta Theta chapter of Gamma Phil Delta sorority.

Armstrong, a graduate of Lincoln High School, will the honoree at the business and professional women's organization's sixth annual "This is Your Life" banquet at Bally's Grand Hotel.

The event will cover highlights of the life of Armstrong, president and general manager of Ray and Ross Transport, from his childhood through his business accomplishments and contributions to the Las Vegas community. Proceeds go to the sorority's scholarship fund.

Information about the event may be obtained by calling Susan Pence at 702-646-4661.

Although Ray & Ross was excelling and the contributions I was making in the community were fulfilling, I began to go through a lot of back and forth and ups and downs in the business. I know it was all part of the game, and if you want to win, you have to play. However, my doctor couldn't have disagreed with me more.

In 1992, my blood pressure was through the roof, 160/100. Dr. Knoll told me that it was from the stress of my bus business and I needed to get out of it or reduce my hours significantly, if I valued my health. In addition to working long hours, I was stopping by the bar every night for a Seagram's and Coke and I didn't get home until around 1:00 a.m. I had trouble sleeping and I thought the alcohol would help, not thinking that the two-way radio I had on the nightstand next to my bed in case of an emergency might have played a role in it. After getting little or no sleep, by 5:00 a.m., I was in my car headed to work.

When I met with Dr. Knoll in 1998, my vitals were worse. He politely gave me a copy of my file and said, "These are yours. Don't come back to see me until you get out of the bus business. Find another doctor to die on because you are not going to die on my watch."

My personal life wasn't doing much better. As hard as it was for me, I signed the papers that finalized my divorce from Marilyn. The courts ordered me to pay her cash up front for her share in Ray & Ross, but I didn't have it. I did, however, agree to pay her a percentage when and if the company was sold.

# One Day At A Time

"Help me to believe in
what I could be,
and all that I am. Show me the
stairway I have to climb Lord,
for my sake, teach me to take
one day at a time."
— Unknown

# CHAPTER NINE
## SHIFTING GEARS

There was a lot going on in both my personal and business life, but I still found time to attend the Lincoln High School reunion which was held in Las Vegas. Seeing former classmates after so many years made me realize just how far I had come since I left school.

I was nervous and excited when I walked in the hotel lobby. I recognized most of my classmates and I could only hope they knew who I was. I knew I had nothing to prove; I was just happy to see everyone. It brought me back to my childhood.

# Lincoln High School Reunion in Las Vegas

L-R: Susan Jackson, Ida Nell Cook, Flora Kidd, Louis Winfrey, Earnice Shannon, Mary Ann Brown, Francella Sanders, Nora Turner, Barbara Henton, and Frances Johnson

F-L: Joe Smith, Melvin Mann, Calvin Wesley, Herman Green, Dewey Wright, James Todd, Eugene Hawkins, and Melvin Willingham. B-L: Charles Taylor, Billy Randle, Edward Cornelius, Charles Reed, and Theotis Phillips

I was able to spend quality time with just about everyone who attended the reunion. We picked up where we left off several decades ago, which was really surprising to me.

Although I was still hurting from my divorce and my feelings of failure, I decided to date a young lady named Nedra. She had two kids. Her daughter, Morenike Renee was in college, and son Moneer Abdullah was a senior in high school. I knew she was a keeper but because my mind was going in so many directions, I wasn't sure how to handle the relationship. She was the kind of woman who would eventually want to move things to the next level, but I wasn't ready for that and I wasn't sure if I ever would be.

On the other hand, I was ready to build my first house. I sold the one on Brady (bought it for $12,000 and sold it for $190,000) and purchased three-quarters of an acre of vacant land on the corner of El Camino and Russell Road in Southwest Las Vegas. I hired an architect and a contractor out of Louisiana who had experience in building the type of house I always envisioned.

My first custom built house on
El Camino & Russell Road

I wanted a specific texture on the ceiling that only two
UNLV art students were able to create

During the construction phase, I rented a condominium until it was time to move in, which was about a year later.

I wanted a certain type of ceiling and since the builder had no experience in doing the one I requested, he hired a contractor out of Reno. I also wanted a specific texture of paint on it so he called the UNLV Art Department and hired two students. They knew the only way to get that result, a sponge not a brush would have to be used.

In May of 1996, the house was ready. Nedra was in my life so much, I decided to ask for her hand in marriage. I had a special ring made with the words "Love Forever" inscribed inside because she was a woman I had grown to admire and respect.

We wanted our wedding to be a surprise and because it was around Christmas time, we sent out invites for a holiday party with a western wear theme. It was held in a reception hall that was located not too far from the house, and the moment they walked in, a large sign read, "Sam's & Nedra's Saloon."

Sam and Nedra at their wedding

I flew in my friend from Chicago, Reverend James T. Meeks, and his wife, First Lady Jemell to officiate the ceremony. He is the pastor of Salem Baptist Church, and it has one of the largest congregations in Chicago with a membership of over 9,000 and 10 ministries.

Reverend Meeks would later become an Illinois Senator (2003-2013) representing the 15th district and for a short period, he worked with President Obama, who was at that time the Senator for the 13th district.

L-R: First Lady Jemell Meeks, me, Nedra,
and Reverend James T. Meeks

In 1991, when I owned Armstrong's Travel, the primary objective was to be the only travel agency in Las Vegas to organize Holy Land Tours and offer package deals to "mega-churches" and our targeted market was the Black community. We operated out of Ray & Ross Transport offices for many years and employed three travel agents.

One of our largest tour groups was Reverend Meek's church, Salem Baptist. This is how I became acquainted with him. The other was Sweet Holy Spirit which was also in Chicago. Dr. Bishop Larry Trotter is the founder and the pastor of this congregation which consist of 8,000 members.

Armstrong's Travel was also under contract to arrange airline travel for the present governor of Nevada and state employees to and from Reno, Nevada.

At the wedding reception, as soon as the music went off and there was silence, I was nervous as hell. I wondered if I should have told some of the people what was going on but it didn't matter now. When Reverend Meeks announced the reason why everyone was gathered on this day, our guests were very happy we decided to share it with them.

Far L: Nedra's father Bill Cooper

L-R:
Nedra's kids
Moneer and
Morenike

I was really pleased with the results of my first custom built home, but I started to realize that although it was zoned for horses, there just wasn't enough room for what I wanted to do with it. So I purchased a 5-acre property in the Northwest area of the Las Vegas Valley located on Farm Road and Torrey Pines. I wanted it to be a working horse ranch, and I had no plans to live there.

A few years after we were settled in, I woke up one morning and discovered that Russell Road was going to be paved. Suddenly, my quiet surroundings were about to be replaced with a very busy thoroughfare. I started to have second thoughts and I worried that my plans of owning a few horses was definitely out of the question.

## TEST SITE SHUTS DOWN

Like all good things, they eventually come to an end. In 1999, the Nevada Test Site announced they would no longer conduct nuclear testing. And just like that, we were lost. They were our largest income producer and our only contract.

Doug and I had not a clue as to what we should do next. We continued to book interstate charters but the nature of that business was changing, and not in our favor as the Interstate Commerce Commission ceased to exist. We also booked local sight-seeing tours, staging as many as we could even on a per-passenger basis.

We began to shift our focus much more heavily toward providing airport transfers, including the mini-buses. When I asked a representative with the Public Service Commission if my Certificate covered those services, he told me it did. To confuse the situation, the PSC received a complaint from Gray Line alleging that Ray & Ross did not have a Certificate for airport transfers and mini-buses. The PSC changed their mind and agreed to shut us down for that particular Certificate but not all of them.

The one Black-owned company on the airport was a long-standing limousine service, so I guess there was not going to room made for another... Without that one Certificate, we weren't generating enough revenue. We just couldn't see any way out of this. So there was only one thing to do-sell Ray & Ross. But in order to do that, I had to pay Marilyn what was owed to her from the divorce settlement. My partner Doug was okay with me grabbing the reins to not just ride this situation out, but to rise above all the confusion.

I decided to sell my house on El Camino for $500,000, and made a $400,000 profit. After I settled my debt with Marilyn, I was anxious to get back in the game.

Even in the midst of a storm, I continued to make plans to build a second custom home on the five acres I had bought on Farm Road. And since my health complications dictated that a long daily drive was not a good idea, I placed a manufactured house on the property for Nedra and me to live in.

I hired the architect Sid Green to design the house. When the plans were finalized, the front was located on Donald Nelson Avenue, so that became our address. Nedra thought the master bedroom and bathroom were too small, and because I wanted her to be happy, I asked Sid to revise them to her liking. When the house was completed, I bought a mare and named her Star, and later I bought another one, Princess for Nedra.

In the meantime, my drinking was starting to become excessive. And although it was starting to cloud my thinking, I still thought enough to surprise her with a brand new Mercedes Benz that I paid cash for.

We named our new place the Rock-N-A Ranch, and designed and built a "Mare's Motel" big enough to house 30 horses, and a big barn for hay & equipment. We offered riding lessons and horse breaking and training as well as boarding. There was a school for Special Needs Students not too far from the house and every so often, we would take the horses down there and offer therapeutic horseback riding for the students.

Our Ranch also served as the "home" for the Buffalo Soldiers, who all boarded their horses there. We even built a clubhouse and an outdoor kitchen where we held fundraisers for the Las Vegas Chapter.

# CHAPTER TEN
## BUFFALO SOLDIER
### Fighting on arrival, fighting for survival

L ife on Farm Road had many benefits. I taught my friend Al Crosby how to ride a horse and then he decided to buy one. We both craved to roam the land like a bunch of cowboys but we were unable to find a Black group that was dedicated to that type of lifestyle in Las Vegas.

One day, a friend told me that the 9th & 10th Cavalry Buffalo Soldiers were a group of Blacks who rode horses and that they had 40 chapters throughout the country but none was ever established in Nevada. After asking around,

I found out that two original Buffalo Soldiers lived in Las Vegas.

Trooper Harold Cole was the former National President of the Buffalo Soldiers Associations chapter. I decided to play a few rounds of golf with him and he mentioned that the other original soldier was Trooper Thomas Leigh. I met with him and he was more than willing to help organize and form a chapter in Las Vegas. The meetings took place at my house, and in 2004, we officially formed the Las Vegas Chapter Buffalo Soldiers 9th & 10th Horse Cavalry with 12 members.

One of our chapter's missions was to educate the community, especially the kids, about the sacrifices and the history of these brave soldiers. We would go out to the schools and teach the history and when we brought the horses on the school grounds, about 90% had never seen a horse up close, let alone been on one.

The kids had no idea the Buffalo Soldiers even existed. And how would they, it was a part of our history that was conveniently left out of the school books. They

Greater Las Vegas Chapter Buffalo Soldiers 9th & 10th Cavalry original founding members. L-R: Albert L. Crosby, Louis Conner, Harold Cole, Floyd Brown, me, Don Shumate, and Billy Thomas

Buffalo Soldiers Annual Convention with new young recruits

were surprised to learn that Black men served in the military during that time, in 1866, and that the Native American Indians gave them their name because they had dark, curly hair and fighting power that reminded them of the fierce Buffalo. This was interesting in itself because the main reason the soldiers were organized was to help control the Native Americans, and everything else.

They had to capture cattle rustlers and thieves, and protect settlers, stagecoaches, wagon trains and railroad crews along the Western front. In other words, they fought the Indians and crooks to protect the areas and they were commissioned to clean up the West by any means necessary. But regardless of the many battles they fought and won in brutal weather conditions (San Juan Hill, El Chaney, and Las Guasimas) they faced blatant racism but continued to fight with courage and no fear.

Buffalo Soldiers served among the Nation's first Park Rangers and one of their assignments was Yosemite National Park. During the Spanish-American War, they rode along the side of President Theodore Roosevelt's "Rough Riders" and charged up San Juan Hill, Cuba. They helped win the war, and the President praised them for their service and referred to them as "Guards of Honor."

Our house on Farm Road was spacious enough to sponsor Buffalo Soldier events and conduct hayrides for the kids. I think I enjoyed them more than they did.

Buffalo Soldiers visit Bridger Middle School

A brief introduction to my horses Star and Princess

During the COVID-19 pandemic, the Las Vegas Chapter, Buffalo Soldiers 9th & 10th Cavalry paused all social events and gatherings. But now that things are starting to get back on track, we plan to continue educating the community about the legacy of these tough soldiers who never received the credit they deserved during their time of service.

# CHAPTER ELEVEN
## EVEN RAY & ROSS HAD A PRICE

For years, I was the only Black bus company owner who was a member of the American Bus Association. And whenever I attended a convention, there would be two other Blacks in the attendance who were employees of other member companies, and one was named Steven Slade.

Slade was from the East Coast and had recently moved to Las Vegas. He was close friends with an executive at the Bellagio Hotel and was in charge of conducting the hotel's tours that is until the Public Service Commission found out. He came to me to ask if he could operate under my license, but I declined.

Slade disappeared for about three years, and when he resurfaced, he asked if I was interested in selling Ray & Ross. When I told him that it was definitely up for sale, he arranged for me to meet a White Memphis financial advisor named David Namer.

The first meeting with Namer was cordial but I decided to hire Booker Evans, a Black attorney, to help broker the deal. He was a friend of my close friend, Bob Conner.

Booker was the manager of a local law firm, and the negotiator assigned to my case was a young White lawyer who was fresh out of law school. He advised me to look closer at the offer Namer had on the table and that he was not in favor of it. Bob Conner also said that I should be careful with the deal. On the other hand, Booker said that he had it under control and not to worry. Those responses should have been enough for me to fall back but I had too much on my plate that I needed to resolve and with a quickness.

During the second meeting, I left shortly after it started. I simply had a bad feeling about the whole thing. I told Booker the deal was off, that I couldn't deal with Namer, and that it wasn't a good time. I was the President of Vusamart American Sight-Seeing International, which is an organization of sight-seeing companies. Their convention was being held in Southern California and I was in the middle of organizing a few things in order to attend.

While I was at the convention, Booker Evans called and said he was going to replace me as the negotiator because he knew that I refused to deal with Namer plus the guy had yet to be cleared by the Public Service Commission.

As far as the license I acquired from TUI, there were only 12 issued in the State of Nevada and only two went to a bus company, Ray & Ross and LTR. The remaining were issued to hotel presidents for need and necessity. If they could prove it, they were certified.

The Public Service Commission finally told David Namer he wasn't going to be approved. He told them it didn't matter that he was still going to buy the company. So I told my attorney Booker Evans to start the process to sell to him even though originally, Steven Slade was supposed

At the Vusamart I had to prepare for when I walked out of the meeting with Booker Evans and David Namer

L-R: Las Vegas Showgirl, me, Jan (Sales for Las Vegas Convention & Visitors Authority), Richard Valerio (President of American Sightseeing International), and Las Vegas Showgirl

Governor's Conference on Travel & Tourism
L-R: Two representatives of Nevada State Tourism
Commission, Governor Bob Miller, Catherine Cortez
Masto, me, and Erika (Ray & Ross Sales Manager)

Manny Cortez was a long-time friend. He was the lawyer for TUI and President of the Las Vegas Convention & Visitors Authority for 13 years. He would have been proud to see how well his daughter, Senator Catherine Cortez Masto (above) is doing today

to be buying the company. That's when I found out that Slade was acting as a front for Namer.

In December of 1999, my controller brought me a financial statement that proved David Namer had put his name on my company even before he placed a bid. He had submitted it to the federal trade commission and placed it on the New York Stock Exchange before the purchase of the company was complete.

I took the paperwork to my first attorney, Neils Pearson, and he advised me not to go back to them about this, to get out as clean as I could immediately. At the time, Pearson was with a national law firm and he was in the process of obtaining an international license to practice all over the world.

On September 28, 2000, I was informed that Namer was arrested and charged with 93 counts of conspiracy, securities fraud, mail fraud, wire fraud, money laundering, and tax evasion. From 1994 through 1996, he sold approximately $23 million of corporate notes that he represented as insured when there was in fact no insurance in place. The issuers of these notes were the Development

Authority of Mitchell County, Georgia; Tri Star Financial Corporation; Aircraft Leasing and Funding Company, LLC; Northstar Leasing Company, LLC; and Ray & Ross Transport, Inc.

I was told that he sold $6 million of corporate notes of Ray & Ross Transport, Inc., without approval and without informing us. He also diverted a total of $1,975,000 from the proceeds of the Aircraft Leasing, Ray & Ross, and Northstar Leasing note issues to purchase for his own personal benefit. The feds recovered about $28 million but none of it ever filtered down to me. And just like that, I was being investigated by the feds and I didn't even know it.

During Namer's trial, I flew four times to Memphis, Tennessee to testify on my company's behalf. I had no idea what was going on and I couldn't give them any factual information because I didn't have any idea that my company was even involved in this mess.

According to a September 1, 2011, article in The Daily News, a Memphis newspaper entitled "Epilogue in Securities Fraud Case Concludes", Namer was found guilty on August 20, 2002 on all charges and sentenced to 29 years and two months in prison. It was one of the longest white collar sentences in history and the largest securities fraud case ever tried in Memphis federal court. The judge ruled that Namer was a narcissistic sociopath with no empathy for others. Then in 2007, U.S. District Court Judge Bernice Donald reduced his sentence by nine years to an even 20.

The article also stated that two of Namer's lawyers and two judges were disbarred, his four contacts on Wall Street were sentenced and scheduled to go to prison, and that one of them committed suicide.

When I testified against Namer at the trial, I looked at him and all I could see was the image of a snake. But then again, Steven Slade, a brother, was the one responsible for bringing this criminal to the table.

The courts kept me up-to-date on the whereabouts of those convicted in the trial. I had also heard that Slade was arrested and sentenced to five years but only served three, and that he moved back home and was driving a cab. If only I would have listened to that young White lawyer who was fresh out of law school.

I felt Booker Evans was the best lawyer in town and that he was a friend who was going to take care of me and look out for my best interest in every possible way, or so I thought. I never would have imagined in a million years he would stab me in the back. But then again he did have a dark side, and I witnessed it at a dinner held by former Assemblyman Woodrow Wilson's daughter, JoAnn Wilson Conner, the wife of my friend Bob.

Woodrow Wilson was the first Black Nevada State Assemblyman in the State of Nevada. At events and dinner engagements, Booker Evans would always sit at the table with JoAnn and me laughing and talking about everyday matters knowing all along that he was part of a sting that would eventually bring down her father.

In 1984, Wilson's sterling public career was damaged when he became part of a sting deemed Operation Yobo named after former Nevada FBI chief Joseph Yablonsky. He was the only one convicted in the sting but was not required to serve time in prison. Instead, he was given a two-year suspended sentence and three years probation. The Operation's team included four members from the

DA's office and Booker Evans was the only Black lawyer involved in the sting.

Ray & Ross Golf Tournament Award Ceremony
L-R: Raymond Chester, Assemblyman Woodrow Wilson,
and Sandra Scott

Looking back, I realized how cold Evans was to sit at the same table with JoAnn. For three consecutive Saturdays, he came to our homes for dinner, mixing and mingling like he was a true down brother. But even knowing he had this side of him, I still don't think that he intended to harm me. I truly believe he was simply outsmarted.

When I placed Ray & Ross on the market, my asking price was $10 million. Namer agreed and placed the money in a trust account after the deal was closed with a Nevada title company to pay off Ray & Ross' debts, which came to around $7 million. My attorney came to me and convinced me to let them transfer the money to Namer's local attorney's trust fund and I agreed. I later found out that only half of the $10 million was transferred and the other half was "loaned" to Namer.

My negotiator contacted each company Ray & Ross owed and made sure we settled and paid them in full. The total amount paid out was approximately $5 million, instead of $7 million, and now it was time for me to get my cut. According to my agreement with Namer, I was entitled to what was left after all of the bills were paid. But no matter how many calls I made, I got answers but no money. I thought I was going to lose my mind.

When I called Namer's Las Vegas attorney, his secretary said he was on a three month ski trip. And when I called Booker Evans' office, I found out he had transferred to Phoenix, Arizona. I wanted to get both of them together in an office and get revenge.

I was in a very dark place and Nedra knew something was terribly wrong. When she found out what I was thinking, she talked me out of it. She saved me from self destructing, and possibly spared the lives of two men.

It took me two years to find a lawyer to sue Booker Evans because lawyers don't like to sue lawyers. The lawyer who accepted my case was appointed to judgeship so he referred me to an attorney named Richard McKnight. It took him two years to sue the law firm, the insurance company, and Booker Evans for $1 million. The case cost me about $800,000 so I only left out the door with the balance.

I can honestly say that out of all of my awards during my years at Ray & Ross, the two I hold closest to my heart is when I was voted "Minority Small Business Person of the Year" (1985) by the State of Nevada. The other was when the United States American Bus Association needed to vote for the best bus company in the USA, and Ray & Ross was one of the three chosen and the only company recorded as having zero fatalities.

After the dust settled from the trial and the lawsuit, my finances were not getting better. I simply didn't have any income coming in. I had two $100,000 investments that were bringing in $1,000 a month, but then those dried up. I took a loan out on Nedra's car to help us get through this bump in the road, which I later paid back.

I had already taken a $1 million dollar loan on the Farm Road property when the property was worth between $5-$8 million dollars. Then the stock market crashed and the property went into foreclosure, but I was able to sell and clear the debt owed.

By this time, my marriage was in complete shambles and there was no turning back. Nedra packed up her stuff and left, and I put my things in my truck and moved into the Budget Suites.

My room at the Suites was so small, I had trouble sleeping; it affected my claustrophobia. I had some of my personal belongings in there, but I decided to park across the street and sleep in my truck. This little routine of mine went on for about a year.

# CHAPTER TWELVE
# FAMILY IS WHERE THE HEART IS

While flying back and forth for the trial, and as things were starting to come to a conclusion, my health started to decline. I had congestive heart failure, and a year later I had a mini-stroke which was followed by open heart surgery.

In 2000, Dr. Conrad Murray, the same doctor who was sentenced for Michael Jackson's death in 2011, said that I needed to replace some bad arteries. I remembered when my sister Velma had open heart surgery and they had to go back in two days later. I was skeptical but I had little or no choice if I wanted to get better.

I had open heart surgery the old fashioned way, which left a large incision down my chest. Dr. Murray said that I might be good for one year or twenty years but if I would have waited any longer, I might have keeled over while walking down the street.

In 2011, I wasn't ready to get back in the game, but I did feel that it would be a good time to ask for the money I loaned the Seven Seas Bar & Restaurant. I had given them a short term loan and when I enquired about it, the balance was eventually paid.

I have always admired the houses in a community on the Westside called Bonanza Village. They are located on an acre or more of land which allows room to grow, and are zoned for horses. I knew most of the residents and felt it would be the perfect area that would force me to be still, at least for now.

I had kept in touch with a former employee, Victor Ingram, who was on active duty in the Army. When he told me that he was scheduled for a tour in the Persian Gulf War in Iraq, where he would be stationed, I asked if he could purchase a house for me. He had no problem with it.

In 2012, the house cost $250,000. I placed a down payment on it and when the paperwork went through, I immediately moved in. A year later, when Victor returned home from the War, I had the house transferred in my name.

In 2021, I started having symptoms of lightheadedness and swelling. My cardiologist placed a stent in an artery, and about a month later he placed another stent in a different artery. My heart symptoms continued and when I went back to the hospital, I had my aortic valve replaced, which was the same procedure as having open heart surgery but without the long scar. My doctor told me that patients with these issues normally have a pacemaker but I wasn't ready to make a decision at that time.

Six months after I was released from the hospital, my heart symptoms continued and on January 5, 2022, I decided to get a pacemaker. A month later, I was admitted in the hospital due to more heart complications, and a few weeks later, I was readmitted for the same issues. That was in February of 2022, and since that last visit, I have felt great and the results from my check-ups, so far, do not show anything to be concerned about.

# MENDING TO HEAL

I had three sisters who lived in Las Vegas, Ester the oldest, Mattie, and Velma, my substitute mom. My brothers Bobby and Billie didn't move to Las Vegas until after James and me had been settled in for some time. It felt nice having them near, but because I was always so busy, I didn't have time to enjoy them. Honestly, I didn't know what to feel.

I never forgot how Velma took me in when I had that falling out with my dad. So I returned the favor by moving her and her daughter Gwen to Las Vegas.

At first they lived in an apartment but then I purchased a condominium for them on Tropicana and Rainbow. When she told me she sold it and bought a house, I was elated. That was the least I could do because I knew she would never ask me for anything.

Velma worked as a maid at the Tropicana Hotel for 38 years. Before she retired, she fell and broke her leg at a grocery store and was hospitalized for a few months. She

L-R: Henry Walker, and my sisters Eva Mae, and Velma

My sister Ester

received a settlement but then she started to have health problems. She had heart surgery, was diagnosed as anemic and a diabetic. When she was 83 years old, one leg started to swell but the doctor didn't want to take the risk of operating on someone her age. So he gave her medicine to keep her stable, and then she was placed in hospice. She died in 2017. She was buried at Palm Mortuary in Las Vegas.

My sister Mattie moved from El Dorado, Arkansas. She had one daughter and she was raised with me and my siblings as though she was one of us. Ester's two kids, Juanita and Robert, were raised the same way. They had them at such a young age my mom thought it was best to have them under her roof. My mom and Dad raised all of their grandkids up until 1975 when they were old enough to be on their own.

Back home in Camden, Arkansas, the economy was at a stand-still. The only industries were the paper mills, roofing plants, and plants for ammunition. I didn't call home that often because I relied on my sisters to update me on what was going on.

The first time my mother flew on a plane was when she came to see me. The second time was when she came for my wedding to Marilyn.

I tried to talk her into moving to Vegas but she wasn't going to leave my dad. She was 13 when they got married and they were going on 60 years at that time and I had to respect that.

My dad never flew on a plane, and he only left Camden twice. In 1956, my brother W.C. and I drove our dad to Dallas, Texas to watch the Brooklyn Dodgers play the Dallas Eagles. His dream was to see the future Hall of Famers, infielder and outfielder Jackie Robinson; catcher Roy "Campy" Campanella; and pitcher Donald "Don" Drysdale. I never saw him that happy. He even waited after the game to see if he could meet one of his idols and maybe get a signature, but it didn't happen.

It's a good thing he went to that game because at the end of the season, to everyone's surprise, Robinson retired. When his team traded him to the San Francisco Giants he refused. He wanted to retire with the Brooklyn Dodgers.

My mom Annie married my dad George
when she was 13 years old

The second time we took my dad out of Camden was to visit Lisbon, Louisiana. There wasn't much to see and it still only had a few hundred people living there.

When my mom told me my dad's health was failing, I knew to suggest a doctor was out of the question. Folks in the south, especially during the late 60s and early 70s, did not believe in going to the doctor. They felt it was a waste of time because they were either humiliated or refused proper treatment.

One time, my dad went to a White doctor named Dr. Guthrey and he never put his hands on him. So the folks back home learned to heal themselves with remedies like Dr. Tichenor antiseptic and B.C. Powder, which was mixed with castor oil and a shot of whiskey. Then there was powdered Black-Draught which today is a liquid syrup laxative.

Cow Chip Tea and a ball tea, were mostly for kids. After a piece of cloth was soaked in one of the remedies, they would place it around the neck area. It smelled just like cow manure.

My dad was tired from working all those years. He didn't understand that his body was worn down and it was time to listen to what it was saying. He started losing his eyesight and then his teeth, and because he was diabetic, sometimes he had to rely on crutches to walk.

When he died, his burial was scheduled 16 days later, which gave me enough time to find two drivers and get a bus ready to take the family to Camden, Arkansas.

Mom and Dad and one of the twins, Walter, are buried beside each other. Everyone else is located in nearby plots.

I felt sad I didn't resolve the issue I had with my dad when I was in ninth grade. I wished I didn't leave home under those circumstances and I regret not talking to him about it. But then, I doubt he would have had anything to say to me, and it definitely would have taken an enormous effort on both our parts to resolve our disagreement.

Not talking to my dad was my first regret. The others were my divorces from Marilyn and then from Nedra. I had a lot of ups and downs but these I couldn't fix. There was nothing I could have done. To go against what I felt would have eaten me up inside. I never knew how to give in to someone else's way of life.

L-R: Billy, Eva, me, Bobby and Velma

Mom and Dad with grandkids

# EVERYDAY BLESSINGS

One of my favorite artists of all time was the elegant and sophisticated singer and actress, Nancy Wilson. And one of her many songs I learned to love was "(You Don't Know) How Glad I Am." The following excerpt from that song, describes how I feel about my kids.

*I wish I were a poet so that I could express*
*What I, what I like to say*
*I wish I were an artist,*
*So that I could paint a picture*
*Of how I feel, how I feel today*
*My love has no walls on either side,*
*That makes my love wider than wide,*
*I'm in the middle and no and I can't hide loving you*
*And you don't know, you don't know,*
*How glad I am, and you don't know,*
*You don't know, how glad I am,*
*How glad I am.*

All eight of my kids hold a special place in my heart; I continue to claim Nedra's children, Morenike and Moneer, and their children, as though they were my own. They, like the rest of them, check in quite often to give me the latest on what they are doing and to make sure my health is in good standing. I have been blessed to spend time with each and every one of them at family events, which are mostly around the holidays. I say I have eight even though I lost my first daughter, Carmen on February 5, 2003.

Carmen was born on July 27, 1964. After graduating from Rancho High School, she wanted to attend the University of Arizona Tucson to get a Bachelors of Art degree, but I didn't think that was a wise choice because she couldn't make a living doing "what she loved." Besides, most artists I read about died penniless. I suggested she attend UNLV first for one full year and if she didn't like it, then we would come back to the table.

Carmen quit school and came to work for Ray & Ross. But my Executive Assistant Susan Pence told me she was struggling to fit in. Carmen and I talked about it several times but we couldn't come to an agreement. She decided to return to UNLV to study Pre-School Education and found a job at a nearby pre-school. She was working with children with special needs, and although she was happy in her new career, she also came to work for me as a Travel Agent at Armstrong's Travel.

In 1999, Carmen adopted a child. His name is Teh Dejon and he was my fourth grandchild. Teh was born on May 27, 1997, but it's sad to say that Carmen was only in his life for a short time. She passed away due to kidney failure on February 5, 2003. Our hearts were broken and we all still miss her every day. Her cousin, my niece Cynthia Armstrong-Sanders and her husband adopted Teh and raised him as one of their own.

Teh graduated from Cheyenne High School in 2005. His interest is in becoming a heavy equipment mechanic.

Right before I started dating Marilyn, and before Carmen, I was with a lady named Grace. She had my first-born, Douglas Ross. And although he resides in the Los Angeles area, we have maintained a very close relationship. After graduating from high school, he served our country in the Marine Corps. Following his honorable discharge in

1989, he joined the Los Angeles Metropolitan Police Department (LAPD). He married Gloria Elaine Kingsberry on March 21, 1993, but they later divorced. Then he married Kimberly (Kim) Yvette in 2012. When he retired from the LAPD in 2018, his rank was Sergeant.

Doug gave me my first two grandchildren: Devin Marquis and Azjah Maria. Devin was born on December 18, 1989. He graduated from Inglewood High school in 2007, and has been serving our country in the U.S. Army since 2013. Azjah was born on May 18, 1996. She graduated from View Park Charter School, and then from the University of Oregon in 2018 with a Bachelor of Science Degree in Business and Sociology.

Marilyn had my second daughter and third child on March 11, 1970. We named her Dusti Nicole. She graduated from Arizona State University with a Bachelor of Arts Degree in Broadcast Communications. On July 9, 1996, she had my grandson Kobe. He graduated from Southern Arkansas University in 2019 with a Bachelor of Arts Degree in Mass Communications.

A few years later came another daughter named Sami Nishon, who was born on June 12, 1972. She goes by "Nikki". She attended Memphis State University on a volleyball scholarship, where she earned her Bachelor of Science in 1994, and a Master of Science in 1995. She wanted to pursue a doctoral degree in Education but I convinced her to change it to Law. In 1999, she earned a Juris Doctorate from the University of Tennessee at Knoxville Law School. When she returned to Las Vegas, she passed the bar exam and became a lawyer.

On March 19, 1999, Nikki had her firstborn, Quentin Maurice. He earned his Bachelor of Science in Education from the University of Tennessee at Knoxville in 2021.

Nikki's younger sister Kisha Roberta was born on February 18, 1974. She attended Morgan State University on an educational scholarship and graduated in 1996 with a Bachelor of Science in Marketing. She gave me twin grandsons, Jonathan Maxwell and Kyle Robert on September 20, 2007.

And 15 years later, I had my last, sixth child, a daughter named Mickail Leigh, born on November 14,

1992. She goes by "Mikki". She graduated from the University of North Carolina at Charlotte in 2015 with a Bachelor of Science Degree in Psychology.

I love my children, and my seven grandkids are sweet, adorable, and all grown up. They mean the world to me. They light up my life and their hugs are amazing, warm, and priceless.

All I want for each of them is to live their best life, and to know that family, friends, and giving back to your community is where you find real meaning.

Doug's LAPD Retirement Announcement

L-R: Chavi, me, Doug, Azjah, Devin, and Kim at
Doug's LAPD Retirement Party

L-R: Sam, Azjah,
Kim, and Doug at
Azjah's graduation
from the University
of Oregon

Carmen
graduated from
Rancho High
School

She attended the
University of
Nevada, Las
Vegas

Carmen and boyfriend Ken at my wedding to Nedra

Dusti graduated
from Arizona
State University

Marilyn and
me at Dusti's
wedding

Sami "Nikki" at
Debutante Ball

She earned a
Juris
Doctorate
from the
University of
Tennessee at
Knoxville
Law School

Kisha at
Debutante Ball

She graduated
from Morgan
State University

L-R: Kisha, Quentin, Nikki, and twins Kyle and Jonathan

Mickail "Mikki" graduated from the University of North Carolina at Charlotte

Mikki recently made a surprise visit to see me

L-R: Jason, Kobe, and Dusti at his graduation from Southern Arkansas University

L-R: Quentin, Nikki, and Celese Rayford Gordon at his graduation from Advanced Technologies Academy

He graduated from the University of Tennessee at Knoxville

Kobe hanging out with grandpa after a family gathering around the Christmas holiday

L-R: Teh, Marilyn, Kobe, and me at Kobe's 21st birthday party

Front L-R: Kyle, Jonathan, (back) Quentin, me and
Maxine at Red Robin Restaurant

Front L-R: Kyle, Jonathan, (back) Kisha,
me and Quentin

# CHAPTER THIRTEEN
# THE ROAD I HAVE YET TO TRAVEL

Ray & Ross Transport, Inc. was built because a White man said that I couldn't do it. He was the head of the Public Service Commission Enforcement Division. When I told him about my bus, he said that he knew I had one and that it was out there running illegally. I told him that was the reason I wanted to see him, to find out what I could and could not do. He said, "Boy...the only thing you can do with that bus in Las Vegas is sell it." It pissed me off but it motivated me more. I thanked him and said, "I bet you that when you're gone, I'll still be here." Ever since I spoke those words, he would write my company tickets for the most trivial things.

When I started R&R, my intention was not to make a bunch of money, but to create an extended family atmosphere within the company and provide an opportunity for our youth who had attended college. I am pleased to see former employees do so well in their careers. I couldn't be more proud of: City Councilman Ward 5 and mayor hopeful, Cedric Crear; former Commissioner District D, Lawrence Weekly; and co-founder and publisher of "Black Image" magazine, Kimberly Bailey-Tureaud.

## TAKE IT EASY...NO WAY

I had planned to do as little as possible. My health is a result of running the bus company non-stop for all those years, heavy drinking, and little to no rest. But when I witnessed the horrific crime of George Floyd Jr. on television, I couldn't keep still.

I organized a protest march called "Seniors United Car Rally" even though I stopped driving a long time ago. By driving small vehicles, we were able to join the protest marchers and show support. I passed out flyers and printed on the front my mission statement which said that we should recognize past and present disparities of the criminal justice system, and to support our youth in fighting for social justice in hopes of a better future. What happened to George Floyd could happen to any Black man at any given moment.

It was Martin Luther King Jr. who said:

"If You Can't Fly Then Run.
If You Can't Run Then Walk.
If you Can't Walk Then Crawl.
But Whatever You Do, You Have
TO KEEP MOVING FORWARD."

For quite some time, I had been keeping my eye on a 27–acre undeveloped site located along Carey Avenue between Revere and Commerce streets. I owned 1.5-acres on the corner of Revere and Carey but the vision I had for the large piece of land did not include my property.

At least three different contractors tried to build houses there, but after running into problems with caliche and other unstable soil issues the project was deemed not feasible. And although it's in North Las Vegas, I consider that area to be part of the "Historic Westside" community.

I met with my long-time friend Scotty Johnson, the Quality Control Manager for Richardson Construction and he was definitely interested in pursuing a potential builder for the vacant land and felt that it has been vacant for way too long.

In 2017, Scotty and I started negotiations with North Las Vegas City Councilwoman Pamela Goynes-Brown to find out if we could make something work on that property. After many starts and delays, we finally found a home-builder willing to work with us, KB Home.

After KB purchased the property for around $3.1 million, they proved to be professional and displayed quality work from the start to the finish. During the construction phase, there were 250 families on the waiting list. Today, the Desert Mesa Community is no longer an eyesore. The 123-single-family modern houses are surrounded by natural beauty landscape, and the area is so incredibly inviting, a few political figures decided to make it their home.

We made an effort to ensure that the ongoing integrity of the neighborhood continues by including in the

CC&Rs (Covenants, Conditions, and Restrictions) that the houses could only be sold to owner/residents, not to corporations or other investment entities. Every so often, I take a drive through the neighborhood just to make sure it continues to look beautiful and well kept. In my opinion, it's one of the nicest neighborhoods in the Historic Westside.

After the homes were built, I managed to maintain ownership of my 1.5 acres of land on the corner of Carey and Revere. Scotty and I wanted to build a convenience store with gas pumps, but Councilwoman Goynes-Brown would not approve it. In her opinion, that would attract an undesirable element to the area. At first I didn't understand her reason for saying that, but later I did and I agreed with her assessment.

About a year ago, I was approached by a developer who had built strip malls all over the country. He was interested in my property and we were able to negotiate a purchase price. Presently, there is a retail complex that stands on my "used to be" property that will consist of stores and restaurants in one long building. I look forward to the grand opening.

It's been 20 years since that area has seen a new strip mall. And I hope it won't take that long for another one to be developed on a corner in the community.

I refused to let bad investments, loss of my business, and a sudden decline in my health, stop me from fulfilling my purpose on earth. I never tried to prove anything; I just wanted to be a witness to my trials and tribulations so that I could one day pass on the lessons learned. Although I didn't achieve all my dreams, I would not have received any of the few I was blessed with if I didn't at least try.

## TOO BLESSED TO BE STRESSED

Today, I am blessed with two 12 hour a day assistants, a nurse and a personal caregiver. I have physical therapy on several machines and I work with weights at least three days a week. My vitals are checked to make sure I am staying on track and ever since I was given a pacemaker, I have not had a bad day.

I go to bed around 11:30 p.m. and get up around 4:30 a.m. just like I did when I was reporting for duty at Ray & Ross. My diet includes less sodium, and to eat healthier, I planted mustard greens, corn, okra, onions, sweet potatoes and just about all of the seasoning herbs you can recall in my garden.

What I know for sure is that it is a blessing to be able to get up every day and be alive. All of my problems made me closer to God, my one true source I always turn to when I need advice. This little boy from Camden, Arkansas, by way of Lisbon, accomplished a lot from all my hard work. It might not have turned out the way I pictured it, but at least my intentions were good and hopefully the world is a better place because of them.

There are a few areas, however, where I wished I could have contributed more. One is to enhance race relations. The other is to influence more young Blacks to get a law degree and then become involved in politics. Being in a position to change the laws will create change for the better for not just our people, but for all people.

In support of my belief, I am in the process of creating the Armstrong Family and Associates Foundation, a non-profit program. The Foundation will reward scholarships for inner-city students who have demonstrated academic leadership and concern for their community and a desire to attend a Historical Black College. I also plan to provide a 12-week Summer Internship. My mission is to empower and enrich their lives through education and prepare them for community service and leadership.

A few years ago, I received a lengthy letter from a former Ray & Ross employee. His name is Reginald "Reggie" Reese and he was once voted my "#1 Driver Trainer." The words he chose to describe how honored he was to work for me and Doug and the positive impact it had on his career, were so moving, I felt compelled to share just a few sections. There are awards and there are rewards.

Reginald Reese
Former
Ray & Ross
Employee

**In his letter, he wrote:**

*You believed you saw something in me that was valuable and gave me a chance. You allowed me to train your most valuable commodity, your employees. I did not fully understand the philosophy of "non-paid, eight week" training. I hated going through it and was empathetic when trainees had to drop out due to financial hardships.*

*From you, I learned the value of keeping only the ones who wanted it more than anyone else. We'd start with 20 trainees and end up with 5 (if we were lucky) graduates. But those we kept were usually the best of the best. They had (for the most part) our values and understood that their performance meant our success and paychecks. I do remember when someone was responsible for losing a major account once, and how lean it got for a while. I taught that in training class and never forgot it.*

*My father passed away the week of Christmas 2015. He was one of the few heroes I have had in my life. You and Mr. McCain are among those left. It was a blessing that I was able to tell my dad how much I loved and appreciated him. I thought I would reach out to my other heroes and tell them how much I admire them, and thank them for what they have done for me. No matter where I go or what I do, I will always be proud of Ray & Ross. If there is ever anything I can do for either of you at this time in this life, I would be honored if you would call on me. Thank you both and may God bless you.*

*Sincerely,*
*Reginald C. Reese*
*Chief Safety Officer*
*Pierce Transit*

Me at 28 years old

# LEGACY

I have been recognized by politicians, corporations, and distinguished citizens for my efforts. I have so many plaques and frames on my walls I have ran out of space.

The other day, I was listening to the radio and I heard a song by blues legend, Tyrone Davis. It was called, "Gone Tomorrow, Here Today" and it was dedicated to his beloved friend, legendary blues singer, Johnnie Taylor. The lyrics towards the end perfectly described how I felt when I said goodbye to Ray & Ross Transport.

*Some tried to copy your emotions*
*To labor your style with things untrue*
*But you jacked your pants up and told them*
*You still call it the blues*
*You gave so much love to the world*
*And expressed it with every song*
*You gave your legacy to the world*
*That will always live on*
*We love you, yes we love you*

And as far as what my legacy will be?

It is yet to be written.

**—TO BE CONTINUED...—**

# Books/Bibliographies/Websites

Buffalo Soldiers
History.com Editors
December 7, 2017
https://www.history.com/topics/westward-expansion/buffalo-soldiers

## Newspapers

Dill Dries, "Epilogue in Securities Fraud Case Concludes" (<u>The Daily News</u> a Memphis newspaper, Vol. 126 | Thursday, September 1, 2011)

## Pictures Courtesy of

Sammie "Sam" Armstrong Family Collection

Gary Thompson, "Black History Demonstration" (<u>Las Vegas Review Journal</u> | May 2, 1992)

J.D. Morris, "Former L.V. mayor spotlights glaring lack of women in top gaming jobs" (<u>Las Vegas Sun Inc.</u> | Thursday, June 9, 2016)

F. Andrew Taylor, "Elementary School named for LVCVA legend Manny Cortez", (<u>Las Vegas Review Journal</u> | February 7, 2012)

# Appointed Positions & Awards
## Just to name a few...

American Bus Association Board Member

Board's Student Activity Committee

Boys' and Girls' Clubs of Las Vegas Board Member

Business and Economic Development Award, NAACP

Chairman of the American Sightseeing International

Chairman of the Clark County School District
  Transportation Safety Council

Clark County School District Advisory Member

Clark County School District's Comprehensive Master
  Plan

Commissioner of the Housing Authority of the City of
  Las Vegas

Community College of Southern Nevada Advisory
  Board Member

Crossing Guard Services in Clark County, Co-founder

Deputy Constable City of Las Vegas & North Las
  Vegas
Distinguished Service Award
Governor's Conference BED Appointee
Las Vegas Chapter of the National Forum of Black
    Public Administrators, instrumental in starting
Latin Chamber of Commerce Advisory Board Member
Minority Small Business Person of the Year-1985
Owner of Armstrong Travel
PepsiCo, Inc. Second Black employee, Clark County
Pop Warner Football Coach
President of VUSAMART
This Is Your Life, Gamma Phi Delta Sorority-1987
United Bus Owners Advisory Board
UNLV Rebel Booster

"May the road rise up to meet you and the wind be ever at your back and may the Lord hold you in the hollow of His hand"
— Anonymous

Made in the USA
Columbia, SC
22 December 2022

8b1ff05f-d244-4534-856b-ffba660f5361R01